De-Moralizing Gay Rights

Cyril Ghosh

De-Moralizing Gay Rights

Some Queer Remarks on LGBT+ Rights Politics in the US

palgrave
macmillan

Cyril Ghosh
Wagner College
Staten Island, NY, USA

ISBN 978-3-319-78839-5 ISBN 978-3-319-78840-1 (eBook)
https://doi.org/10.1007/978-3-319-78840-1

Library of Congress Control Number: 2018937868

Printed on acid-free paper

This Palgrave Pivot imprint is published by the registered company Springer International Publishing AG part of Springer Nature
The registered company address is: Gewerbestrasse 11, 6330 Cham, Switzerland

Nein, es ist für mich.

Acknowledgements

The title of this book is derived from the title of Part One of Elizabeth Brake's *Minimizing Marriage: Marriage, Morality, and the Law* (Oxford: Oxford University Press, 2012): "De-Moralizing Marriage." I owe Brake a debt of gratitude for this clever pun.

Many thanks to Michelle Chen, John Stegner, and Azarudeen Ahamed Sheriff at Palgrave for their patience, encouraging words, and cooperation throughout the process of my writing this book.

For various forms of help, including but not limited to their critiques, their insights, and/or their editorial assistance, I thank B. Lee Aultman, Payal Banerjee, Sandeep Banerjee, Oliver Basu Mallick, Keith J. Bybee, Elizabeth F. Cohen, Gordon Danning, Nicholas Ealy, Leonard Feldman, Beatrice Banee Ghosh, Shaohua Hu, Jyothin Joshi, Portia Joshi, Jeffrey Kraus, Lily H. M. Ling, Atreyee Majumder, Chapal Mehra, Shane O'Brien, Everita Silina, Curtis Wright, and the members of my Spring 2018 graduate seminar on "International LGBT+ Rights" at The New School.

EFC: for rupturing *jus sanguinis*. Shanester: for every day.

All errors in the work that follows are mine.

Contents

1 De-Moralizing Gay Rights 1

2 Radical Theory Creep 11

3 *Obergefell v. Hodges*: Marriage Equality's Insistence on Family Values 43

4 Covering's Other Hidden Assault 73

5 Epilogue 95

Appendix 99

Index 109

CHAPTER 1

De-Moralizing Gay Rights

Abstract In this introductory chapter, I synopsize the argument of the book. In so doing, I begin by pointing out that this book is intended as a polemic. I then delineate the argument in what follows. This book critically interrogates three sets of distortions in twenty-first century public discourse on LGBT+ rights in the United States. The first relates to the critique of pinkwashing, often advanced by scholars who claim to be proponents of a radical politics. I suggest that this critique sometimes suffers from analytical overreach. The second concerns a recent US Supreme Court decision, *Obergefell v. Hodges* (2015), a judgment that established marriage equality across the 50 states. I argue that this judgment mobilizes the Court's own endorsement of two elements of homonormativity: amatonormativity and repronormativity. Instead of endorsing homonormativity, the Court should have instead employed an approach based on decisional minimalism. The third distortion occurs in Kenji Yoshino's theorization of the concept of gay covering. Yoshino's calls to dismantle cultural demands for gay covering turn out, I argue, to constitute an oppressive command to "gay-flaunt."

Keywords Amatonormativity · Covering · Homonormativity
Repronormativity · Marriage equality · Pinkwashing · Queer theory

C. Ghosh, *De-Moralizing Gay Rights*,
https://doi.org/10.1007/978-3-319-78840-1_1

1.1 Introduction

This book is intended as a polemic. It takes issue with a critical distortion rife in twenty-first century public discourse on LGBT+ rights in the United States.[1] The distortion relates to the category of the "queer" and is mobilized by both mainstream, good-hearted liberals as well as by those who more closely identify as queer and/or radical. It typically functions through the public articulation of a series of assimilationist and identity-stabilizing injunctions deployed in order to underwrite a presumptive gay rights *program* decided—apparently—in advance of any contestation.

These injunctions track what Lee Edelman—in offering a critique of the dominant mainstream's obsession with children—has called "an ideological Möbius strip" that has a "'self-evident' one-sidedness" (Edelman 2004, 2). They also reproduce the following binary logic: you-agree-with-us-therefore-you-are-enlightended-versus-you-disagree-with-us-therefore-you-must-be-benighted. Ostensibly deployed in the name of LGBT+ rights, each of these binary logics is a modern-day American Jeremiad (Bercovitch 1978) steeped in a deeply moralizing rhetoric and each consummately misrecognizes the category of the queer.[2] They do so by either dismissing the queer positions on the subject of their inquiry or by rendering these positions invisible or inferior (Young 1990, especially 58–61).

In this book, I critically interrogate three paradigmatic sets of such injunctions frequently cited in contemporary LGBT+ rights discourse. The first relates to the critique of pinkwashing, often advanced by scholars who claim to be proponents of a radical and emancipatory politics. The second concerns a recent US Supreme Court decision, *Obergefell v. Hodges*, in which the majority opinion—one that established marriage equality across the 50 states—is wholeheartedly committed to encoding into the law of the land the Court's own endorsement of two central elements of homonormativity: amatonormativity and repronormativity.[3] The third site of my inquiry is Kenji Yoshino's theorization of the concept of gay covering.[4] In spite of Yoshino's best intentions, his calls to dismantle cultural demands for gay covering turn out to constitute a sanctimonious and oppressive command to "gay-flaunt."

In the remainder of this introductory chapter, I begin in Sect. 1.2 below with a discussion of the specific intervention this book is intended to occasion. Here, I foreshadow some of the ideas that I engage with in greater detail in the empirical chapters of the book. In Sect. 1.3, I provide an outline of the chapters to come. I conclude this introductory chapter with a Note to the Reader that includes some remarks about the different ways in which this book may be read.

1.2 The Nature of the Intervention

When one writes of queer theory one is in fact writing of queer theories. As Berlant and Warner suggest, queer theory "cannot be assimilated into a single discourse" (Berlant and Warner 1995, 343). Its self-conscious deployment as an analytic category—in the service of critique—did not happen overnight or by happenstance. It has a specific historical context. Queer theory developed in the interstices of a conversation in the academy in the early 1990s between scholarship on poststructuralism, on the one hand, and scholarship on gay and lesbian studies (sometimes nowadays also called queer studies), on the other. The latter is properly understood as both a product of, as well as a constitutive element of, a broader set of identity-based social movements clustered under the rubric of the New Left.

By the late 1980s and early 1990s, these kinds of "identity politics," predicated on a politics of separatism and difference, appeared to be ascendant everywhere in the academy. Newly emergent departments, curricula, programs, and institutes dedicated to women's studies, gay and lesbian studies, disability studies, ethnic studies, and so on were but only a few signs that identity politics was flourishing in the corridors of higher education. In the last three decades, in addition to theories of identity politics, a range of related discussions—such as the politics of difference, the politics of recognition, the politics of acknowledgement, multiculturalism, assimilation, integration, diversity, democratic inclusion, and most recently social justice—have become ubiquitous (see, e.g., Young 1990; Phillips 1993; Taylor 1994; Kymlicka 1995; Fraser 1995, 1997; Markell 2003; Fraser and Honneth 2003; Kenny 2004; Wolbrecht and Hero 2005; Ghosh 2013; Heyes 2016).

Queer theory has an uneasy relationship with identity politics. It shares affinities with it as well as resists it. It does the former by dis-identifying—and always preserving a critical distance—from a dominant heterosexual mainstream. But it also resists identity politics to the extent that it rejects the stabilization of any form of identity at all (Berlant and Warner 1995; Jagose 1996). Thus, while gay and lesbian studies has positioned the homosexual body as always outside of, or on the margins of, a dominant mainstream populated by heterosexuals, queer theorists have resisted this inside/outside binary by taking it as axiomatic that it is impossible to locate oneself fully outside the dominant discourse (Namaste 1994, 224; Fuss 1991). The figure of the queer has thus always been without a specific locus: Never fully inside nor fully outside the dominant discursive context, and always politically committed to eradicating the inside/outside, as well as other, binaries.

Indeed, the queer is "constituted through its dissent from the hegemonic, structured relations and meanings of sexuality and gender" (Duggan 2001, 225) and is mobilized to contest the "stability and ineradicability of the hetero/homo hierarchy" (Fuss 1991, 1). Queer theory's foundational insights inhere in the social construction and dis-alignment of sexuality, sex, and gender. Thus, in *The History of Sexuality: Volume I*, Foucault delineates the (reverse-) discursive history that reveals the constructionist character of the homosexual as a "species" (Foucault 1990 [1978], 43). In Foucault's telling, the consolidation of this identity is an artifact of a proliferation of a discourse on sexuality, one that is always already mobilized both in the name of and as a transgression of the Puritan triple edict of "taboo, nonexistence, and silence" (Foucault 1990, 5). Two critical insights to be found here are, first, that a social phenomenon (silence) may sometimes create the condition of possibility for its own negation (verbosity); and second, that there is no identity of the "homosexual" that predates attempts to regulate "homosexuality."

These insights are mirrored in the work of Judith Butler, whose seminal—indeed paradigm-shifting—contribution has been to demonstrate that there is no gender that precedes its regulation and that stands outside of its performance. Butler destabilizes the notion of gender, together with the male–female gender binary on which it is predicated, by pointing out not only that gender is decisively *both* material and performative but also that it is arbitrary, in the sense that there is no such thing as a gender that one is said to *have* outside of a given discursive and interpretive context. This context, in turn, at once regulates the gender being spoken of while also enabling the condition of possibility for its repeal (see, e.g., Butler 1990, 2004). A queer theoretic commitment to unsettle the notion of gender is thus emancipatory because it liberates the sexed object from the pressure of neat alignments. It resists assimilation into any one (pre)scribed ontology. It is open to diverse configurations of sex, desire, anatomy, genitals, gender performance, chromosomes, hormones, gender expression, sex characteristics, sexual orientation, and so on.

But, as Eve Kosofsky Sedgwick describes it in *The Epistemology of the Closet*, these "deconstructive contestations can occur...only in the context of an entire cultural network of normative definitions" (Sedgwick 1990, 11). Such normative definitions are enduring and enjoy widespread legitimacy—that is what a norm is. They are also designed to circumscribe the limits of what they name and make intelligible. Queer theory's oppositional politics is to forever engage in a dialectical contestation that attempts to sunder these normalizing injunctions and make them exceed their normative boundaries. Its political project is, thus, always an ongoing one.

In the analyses that follow, I contribute to the ongoing work of this political project by offering discrete investigations into three sets of normalizing and assimilationist injunctions emanating from the messianic core of contemporary LGBT+ rights politics in the United States. These critiques are intended to do the explicit work of dissenting from the "hegemonic, structured relations" of gender and sexuality that are shored up by the kinds of moralizing rhetoric under interrogation here. It is, however, my sincere hope that the critiques I have offered here are taken in the spirit in which they are offered. In alignment with the eternal commitment of the category of the queer, I stress here that none of the investigations presented in this book intends to speak with an eye toward achieving some kind of finality. Instead, they are each activated here as interruptions to some ongoing monologue that considers its moral superiority to be axiomatic. While these interruptions are indeed intended to foreclose these monologues, they also constitute a call to begin dialogues.

1.3 Outline of the Book

As indicated above, in the three empirical chapters of this book, I use a queer analytic to critically interrogate some of the assimilationist injunctions that lie at the heart of contemporary LGBT+ rights discourse in the United States.

In doing so, in Chapter 2, I investigate some strands of the critique of pinkwashing. In recent years, many radical/queer LGBT+ rights activists have identified pinkwashing as the act of characterizing western democracies as havens of individual rights on the grounds that they are progressive on the question of LGBT+ rights. In the process, pinkwashing demonizes as gross human rights abusers those countries—often Muslim countries—that do not have LGBT+ rights protections. Thus, for example, people like Katherine Franke and Sarah Schulman have correctly suggested that Israel uses its progressive state policies on gay rights as a public relations campaign to throw into sharp relief many Arab and other Muslim-majority countries' record and public stance on gay rights. To be sure, there is a lot to be gained from the political critique that the concept of pinkwashing enables. However, in this chapter, I also suggest that those who accuse western democracies of pinkwashing also sometimes easily slip into a totalizing oppositional politics that attempts to offer a wider critique than their analytic category is capable of producing.

I call this phenomenon Radical Theory Creep. As I show in this chapter, Radical Theory Creep occurs when what begins as a perfectly pointed and systematic critique of one thing—say, for example, US pinkwashing—steadily loses its analytical rigor as the argument develops, usually as a result of it attempting to incorporate within itself a range of other strains of radical/queer theoretic critique. Consequently, each such discursive formation shores up a series of unsustainable conflations and binaries that, in turn, produce their own assimilationist injunctions, albeit not into the mainstream but, instead, into the fold of what is being proffered as a radical and/or queer critique.

In Chapter 3, I critically analyze the legal reasoning that underwrites the US Supreme Court's majority opinion in *Obergefell v. Hodges*, a judgment that in 2015 finally made marriage equality the law of the land in all 50 states. In so doing, I draw upon some critical insights from queer theory. Queer theorists point out the dangers of "normifying" any particular way of life because it demeans and marginalizes those who will not, or cannot, assimilate into the dominant culture. This chapter investigates the assimilationist tropes of amatonormativity and repronormativity in the opinion to point out that it alienates everybody except the most conformist of gays and lesbians. The Court's reasoning is clearly invested in LGBT+ normalization and endorses one particular conception of the good family and the good intimate life. Instead of identifying a specific conception of the good intimate life, and giving it the full support of the state's sovereign endorsement, this decision, I suggest, should have followed an approach steeped in what Cass Sunstein has called "decisional minimalism." Following such an approach would have enhanced, rather than constricted, the range of family formations endorsed by the state in *Obergefell*, and most likely tempered the conflict.

In Chapter 4, I engage with the concept of gay "covering"—a term drawn from the work of Erving Goffmann, and popularized by Kenji Yoshino in the context of LGBT+ rights. Gay covering refers to actions of individuals to "disattend," or tone down, their (despised) sexuality in an effort to fit into and be accepted by the mainstream. In Yoshino's telling, gay covering is the newest iteration of a set of societal (and even legal) injunctions for gays and lesbians, in the beginning, to convert, then, to pass, and finally, to cover. As Yoshino correctly points out, gay covering is motivated by a desire to *belong* to the mainstream but it is also an act that exacts a psychic cost. At the same time, however, he also elides any critical engagement with the question of agency on the part of the subject of covering. Consequently, Yoshino comes across as misunderstanding the plural motivations that may lead an individual to elect to engage in conduct that he characterizes as covering. But these acts of covering, inasmuch as they are that, can be, variously, self-protective, self-affirming, politically motivated, and even politically subversive.

Yoshino's analysis also misreads some forms of conduct as if they encode acts of covering when in fact the individuals performing those acts are potentially merely "being themselves." Because he does not consider this possibility with the seriousness it deserves, the way he mobilizes the analytic category of covering produces a reverse-assimilationist injunction that is analogous to the canard of "acting white." It is not a small irony, therefore, that Yoshino's critique can sometimes end up being just as oppressive as the oppression it is mobilized to dismantle. Consequently, it can harm, rather than help, LGBT+ persons and curtail, rather than enhance, their freedoms.

In investigating these three moralizing and assimilationist rhetorical tropes embedded in articulations about LGBT+ rights emanating from both the state as well as from non-state actors, this book's central contribution is to point out that it behooves LGBT+ rights advocacy and scholarship to take seriously the powerful set of correctives that would issue from a serious engagement with queer theory. Such a gesture would not only throw into sharp relief the need for a continuous re-evaluation of the discursive formations identified in this book as each assembling an oppressive set of assimilationist injunctions. It would also, one hopes, lead to a rupture of these ideological Möbius strips and their self-evident one-sidednesses.

1.4 Note to the Reader

Each of the three topical chapters in this book constitutes a discrete intervention into a particular discursive formation. The book is structured in a way in which the reader has the liberty to read these chapters in a sequential or a non-sequential order, as well as to be selective about which of the chapters they are interested in focusing on or even reading at all. So, for example, a scholar of the US Supreme Court may decide to focus exclusively on Chapter 3 and disregard the remainder of the book. A scholar of social theory might read Chapter 4 more carefully than the other chapters. Someone interested in the concept of LGBT+pinkwashing would be wise to devote their attention to Chapter 2 of the book. And so on and so forth. Each essay represents an independent polemic as well as one example of a number of possible queer contestations of contemporary LGBT+rights rhetoric in the United States.

Notes

1. The abbreviation "LGBT+" represents an "inclusive" way of identifying a range of individuals who do not self-identify as cisgender and heterosexual. See, for example, *BBC Newsbeat* (2015).
2. On the harm of "misrecognition," see, generally, Young (1990) and Fraser (1995, 1997).
3. The two terms, amatonormativity and repronormativity, are relative neologisms. I clarify the two concepts in detail in Chapter 3.
4. There are many forms of covering. I am primarily interested in Yoshino's articulations about gay covering. I explain the meaning of the term in detail in Chapter 4.

References

BBC Newsbeat. 2015. "We Know What LGBT Means but Here's What LGBTQQIAAP Stands for." *BBC News*. June 25. http://www.bbc.co.uk/newsbeat/article/33278165/we-know-what-lgbt-means-but-heres-what-lgbtqqiaap-stands-for.

Bercovitch, Sacvan. 1978. *The American Jeremiad*. Madison, WI: University of Wisconsin Press.

Berlant, Lauren, and Michael Warner. 1995. "What Does Queer Theory Teach Us About X?" *PMLA* 110: 343–349.

Butler, Judith. 1990. *Gender Trouble: Feminism and the Subversion of Identity*. New York: Routledge.

———. 2004. "Gender Regulations." In *Undoing Gender*. New York: Routledge.
Duggan, Lisa. 2001. "Making It Perfectly Queer." In *Theorizing Feminism: Parallel Trends in the Humanities and the Social Sciences*, edited by Anne C. Hermann and Abigail J. Stewart, 215–231. Boulder, CO: Westview Press.
Edelman, Lee. 2004. *No Future: Queer Theory and the Death Drive*. Durham, NC: Duke University Press.
Foucault, Michel. 1990. *History of Sexuality. Vol. 1: An Introduction*. New York: Vintage/Random House.
Fraser, Nancy. 1995. "From Redistribution to Recognition: Dilemmas of Justice in a 'Postsocialist' Age." *New Left Review* 1/212 (July–August): 68–93.
———. 1997. *Justice Interruptus: Critical Reflections on the "Postsocialist" Condition*. New York: Routledge.
Fraser, Nancy, and Axel Honneth. 2003. *Redistribution or Recognition: A Political-Philosophical Exchange*. New York: Verso.
Fuss, Diana. 1991. "Inside/Out." In *Inside/Out: Lesbian Theories, Gay Theories*, edited by Diana Fuss, 1–10. New York: Routledge.
Ghosh, Cyril. 2013. *The Politics of the American Dream: Democratic Inclusion in Contemporary American Political Culture*. New York: Palgrave Macmillan.
Heyes, Cressida. 2016. "Identity Politics." In *The Stanford Encyclopedia of Philosophy*, edited by Edward N. Zalta (Summer). Metaphysics Research Lab, Stanford University. https://plato.stanford.edu/archives/sum2016/entries/identity-politics/.
Jagose, Annamarie. 1996. *Queer Theory: An Introduction*. Melbourne: Melbourne University Press.
Kenny, Michael. 2004. *The Politics of Identity: Liberal Political Theory and the Dilemmas of Difference*. Cambridge, UK: Polity Press.
Kymlicka, Will. 1995. *Multicultural Citizenship: A Liberal Theory of Minority Rights*. Oxford, UK: Clarendon Press.
Markell, Patchen. 2003. *Bound by Recognition*. Princeton, NJ: Princeton University Press.
Namaste, Ki. 1994. "The Politics of Inside/Out: Queer Theory, Poststructuralism, and a Sociological Approach to Sexuality." *Sociological Theory* 12 (2): 220–231.
Phillips, Anne. 1993. *Democracy and Difference*. University Park, PA: The Pennsylvania State University Press.
Sedgwick, Eve Kosofsky. 1990. *Epistemology of the Closet*. Berkeley, CA: University of California Press.
Taylor, Charles. 1994. "The Politics of Recognition." In *Multiculturalism: Examining the Politics of Recognition*, edited by Amy Gutmann. Princeton, NJ: Princeton University Press.
Wolbrecht, Christina, and Rodney E. Hero. 2005. *The Politics of Democratic Inclusion*. Philadelphia: Temple University Press.
Young, Iris Marion. 1990. *Justice and the Politics of Difference*. Princeton, NJ: Princeton University Press.

CHAPTER 2

Radical Theory Creep

Abstract In recent years, many radical/queer LGBT+ rights activists and scholars have identified pinkwashing as the act of characterizing western democracies as havens of individual rights on the grounds that they are progressive on the question of LGBT+ rights. In the process, pinkwashing demonizes as gross human rights abusers those countries—often Muslim countries—that do not have LGBT+ rights protections. There is a lot to be gained from this critique. However, in this chapter, I also suggest that this critique can sometimes slip into what I call Radical Theory Creep. This occurs when what begins as a perfectly pointed and systematic critique of one thing steadily loses its analytical rigor as the argument develops, usually as a result of it attempting to incorporate within itself a range of other strains of radical/queer critique. Consequently, each such discursive formation shores up a series of unsustainable conflations and binaries that, in turn, produce their own assimilationist injunctions.

Keywords Hillary Clinton · Human rights · Imperialism Islamophobia · Israel · Pinkwashing · Radical Theory Creep

2.1 Introduction

In the last decade or so, some theorists and activists have proposed a political critique of what they call LGBT+ "pinkwashing."[1] In the context of LGBT+ rights, pinkwashing denotes a deliberate strategy by some

C. Ghosh, *De-Moralizing Gay Rights*,
https://doi.org/10.1007/978-3-319-78840-1_2

states (and even some non-state actors) to obfuscate their human rights violations by upholding, and drawing the world's attention to, their record on LGBT+ rights. To be sure, there is a lot to be gained from deploying pinkwashing as an analytic category to interrogate these official forms of rhetoric—that appear on the surface to be progressive even as they, as I suggest below, encode new variants of an old justification for colonialism: A civilizing mission. In this chapter, I investigate one facet of this rhetoric and suggest that those who advance the critique of pinkwashing sometimes also run the risk of what I call here Radical Theory Creep.[2] As in the case of its close cousin, Mission Creep, Radical Theory Creep occurs when what starts off as a pointed critique with a narrowly defined scope expands beyond its initial purpose and, consequently, both accomplishes less than what it might have done as well as causes quite a bit of collateral harm.

What this looks like in the case of pinkwashing is this: A scholar or activist will begin a systematic critique of one thing—say, for example, US pinkwashing—and then steadily attempt to incorporate within the ambit of this initial critique a range of other, related, strains of critique, such as, in the case of the US pinkwashing example, associated critiques of capitalism, Islamophobia, and the Global War on Terror. The resulting discursive formation ends up as a totalizing oppositional politics that is noticeably less analytically and methodologically rigorous than the initial critique. It also mobilizes a narrow and somewhat restricted view of what a gay rights[3] affirming discourse can *do* in the world.

Such a singular focus on denoting all endorsements of gay rights that emanate from the United States as somehow oppressive also leads those who engage in this form of Radical Theory Creep to inaugurate a binary logic of their own even as they critique the binary logic embedded in the very act of pinkwashing. As Cynthia Weber describes it, these theorists end up deploying an "antinormative-versus-normative binary logic that reproduces the very antinormative-versus-normative binary logic that [they] investigate" (Weber 2016, 116).

Weber, thus, recognizes the phenomenon even as she refrains from theorizing it. In the remainder of this chapter, I develop *a theory* of Radical Theory Creep by focusing on the category of US pinkwashing as a case study. My hope is that once we have at least a preliminary theory of the phenomenon identified here, we will be able to name and interrogate it in various other domains, and, in so doing, show that Radical Theory Creep both occurs frequently and is extremely harmful. In the context of US pinkwashing, it reduces, even as it reifies, most forms of pro-gay articulations emanating from the United States as one undifferentiated discursive formation—and one that is predicated on a depiction of US foreign policy as simultaneously imperialist, hyper-capitalist, hyper-exploitative, and Islamophobic. As a result of this reification, progressives and radicals are asked to align themselves neatly against any pro-gay rights utterance that is issued by the state.[4] The injunction bears an implicit "shaming" threat. If you refuse to resist the pro-gay rights rhetoric emanating from the United States, you run the risk of being labeled as complicit in US imperialism.

This is problematic for all sorts of reasons, but I address two major causes of concern in this chapter. First, this kind of reductionism presents us with the false dichotomy that suggests we are either on the side of the theorist engaged in Radical Theory Creep or we must be complicit in US imperialism, Islamophobia, the Global War on Terror, and so on. As indicated in Chapter 1, this presents us with an infantilizing and demeaning false binary: you-agree-with-us-therefore-you-are-enlightened-versus-you-disagree-with-us-therefore-you-must-be-benighted. The second cause for concern is that if such critiques are mobilized frequently enough, they run the risk of chilling the speech of our allies. Some people who would normally advance pro-gay rights claims without fear of reproach may now censor their speech on the grounds that they may be falsely accused of reenacting the oppression they are attempting to eradicate. This has harmful consequences for LGBT+ rights around the world.

I begin in Sect. 2.2 below by clarifying what the term pinkwashing means. In Sect. 2.3, I focus more specifically on US pinkwashing and critically interrogate what I call here Radical Theory Creep. As a paradigmatic discussion of this species of critique, I examine, closely, in Sect. 2.4, Hillary Clinton's 2011 "gay rights are human rights" speech at the UN. I argue here that while it is undoubtedly true that this speech is an example of pinkwashing, saying, as some theorists have done, that it is delivered in the interest of advancing a US-backed imperialism or Islamophobia constitutes an egregious act of Radical Theory Creep. I conclude in Sect. 2.5 with a few remarks on the harmful effects of Radical Theory Creep.

2.2 Pinkwashing

Sarah Schulman (Schulman 2011) and Katherine Franke (Franke 2012a)—early popularizers of the concept of pinkwashing[5] in the United States—have suggested that Israel uses its seemingly progressive state policies on gay rights as a public relations tool to throw into sharp relief many Arab and other Muslim-majority countries' stance on gay rights. We know, for example, that in 2005, Israel enlisted the help of American marketing executives to embark on a strategy called "Brand Israel"—that would depict Israel as "relevant and modern" (Schulman 2011). As Schulman describes it, this marketing plan was later expanded to "harness" the gay community (Schulman 2011).

According to Naomi Klein, after the Hamas-majority government was elected into office in 2006, the Israelis began an aggressive and protracted public relations campaign to highlight and contrast Hamas's "fundamentalism" against Israel's "supposed enlightened liberalism" (Surasky 2009). This rebranding effort rested upon a combination of efforts, including enlisting the help of the British advertising firm, Saatchi & Saatchi (Franke 2012a, 6); a Tel Aviv Gay Vibe Float in Chicago's Gay Pride Parade (Franke 2012a, 9); promoting "pink tourism" that characterized Tel Aviv as a "gay mecca" (Franke 2012a, 9)[6]; and the obligatory demonization, by Benjamin Netanyahu, of West Asia as a region where "women are stoned, gays are hanged, Christians are persecuted," and where, "Israel stands out. It is different" (Franke 2012a). Critics, however, have consistently denounced these practices. As Aeyal Gross has suggested: "LGBT rights are used [by Israel] as a fig leaf" (Gross, quoted in Franke [2012a]).

To be sure, Israel is not the only country that has carried out this kind of gay rights branding; in fact, "the pinkwashing critique applies to *all* states" (Franke 2012b, emphasis in the original). As Katherine Franke has described it, Romania, for example, was made to undergo a process of gay rights "credentialization" (Franke 2012a, 25) before it was allowed to accede to the EU. Thus, following complaints from Council of Europe rapporteurs, Romania repealed (not without an internal struggle) Article 200, a 1968 statute that criminalized same-sex intimate conduct in any setting, private or public, and that greatly increased penalties for such acts. Thus, by formally indicating that it had assimilated into a western idea of gay rights, Romania was pinkwashing; it was "performing" a "plausible modernity" (Franke 2012a, 28). In return for Romania's efforts to grant its LGBT+ population rights in a way that was "recognizable" to the EU, it got something in return. The EU would now "look the other way" (Franke 2012a, 30) when it came to Romania's abysmal record on the rights of women and Roma and its CIA "black sites" (Franke 2012a, 29–30). Conversely, therefore, the EU's political strategy itself was an act of pinkwashing, just as much as Romania's own strategy was. In the following section, I turn to a detailed discussion of US pinkwashing.

2.3 US Pinkwashing: Radical Theory Creep in Action

While it is undoubtedly true that official rhetoric emanating from the United States sometimes constitutes pinkwashing, I argue here that this kind of critique is particularly susceptible to Radical Theory Creep. As briefly indicated above, this is a phenomenon in which what begins as a perfectly pointed and systematic critique of one thing—in this case, US pinkwashing—sometimes steadily loses track of its original scope. This happens principally because its progenitors start to attach onto the initial critique a range of other, more diverse, strains of radical/queer theoretic critique. As a result, the analytical category that was originally mobilized with a narrowly defined scope is now asked to do the work of critiquing a much broader range of things. This overreach results in a considerable loss of methodological and analytical rigor, as the analytic category ends up inscribing (and, with each newly appended strain of critique, reinscribing) a series of unsustainable conflations and binaries. These conflations and binaries then produce their own assimilationist injunctions, albeit not into the mainstream but, instead, into the fold of what is being proffered as a radical or queer critique.

Thus, in a 2010 piece in *The Guardian*, Jasbir Puar draws attention to "the contradictions of the multicultural politics of inclusion," wherein she reminds us that colonized people have frequently been asked the Woman Question—How well do you treat your women?—as colonizers have attempted to demonstrate, through the mere asking of this question, colonized peoples' inability to self-govern (Puar 2010). Puar then tell us that the Woman Question is now presented as the Homosexual Question: How well do you treat your homosexuals? This is the "current paradigm" through which a universalized notion of civilization is mobilized. "What is gaining acute force," says Puar, "is the anti-Muslim form that such missionary politics are currently taking" (Puar 2010).

Several discrete moves can be excavated from this set of propositions. The first is the inauguration of the idea of a Homosexual Question as a distinct category of rhetoric. The second is the claim that the Homosexual Question now supplants the Woman Question; indeed, there is a paradigm shift in the way in which a universalized notion of civilization is currently deployed. The third is the idea that this shift constitutes a missionary politics. And the fourth is that these forms of politics are taking an anti-Muslim form.

There are, however, a range of conceptual and logical problems with these articulations. Consider this: The Homosexual Question is invariably the question that is asked, either explicitly or implicitly, when a state is involved in pinkwashing. The intended outcome of a pinkwashing strategy is indeed to establish, often by fiat, a civilizational barometer that measures how well a state treats its homosexuals. Thus, Puar's Homosexual Question is always already insinuated when pinkwashing occurs. But unlike what Puar suggests, pinkwashing may or may not take an anti-Muslim form even though it explicitly asks of the object of its critique the Homosexual Question.

This is not to say that pinkwashing *never takes* an "anti-Muslim form." Israeli pinkwashing, described above in Sect. 2.2, frequently does. But to say, without any qualification, that this is the form that "such missionary politics are currently taking" is to obfuscate the fact that not every instance of pinkwashing is even concerned with a Muslim-majority country or people, and has nothing to do with Islamophobia. Puar is impermissibly collapsing the distinction here between the Homosexual Question and Islamophobia.

In Franke's (Franke 2012a) analysis of the Romanian case discussed above, for example, the EU asks of Romania, the Homosexual Question. But, as we have seen, Romania's repeal of Article 200 was very much an act of pinkwashing—a strategy to formally encode a pro-gay rights posture within the state that asked, implicitly, and in exchange, for the EU to "look the other away" (Franke 2012a, 30) when it came down to Romania's other, somewhat questionable, record on human rights. But, contrary to what Puar insinuates, there is no "anti-Muslim form" to be had here.

Puar's *Guardian* piece is not an isolated example. Here, for instance, are Jasbir Puar and Maya Mikdashi, strenuously reconsolidating the conflation between Islamophobia and pinkwashing, even as they draw in a critique of the US War on Terror: "A myopic focus on Israeli pinkwashing sacrifices a deeper understanding and critique of the ways in which the war on terror, Islamophobia, and rights discourses are intertwined" (Puar and Mikdashi 2012a).

But one must ask: are they? Is this always the case? I raise these questions not because I believe that the war on terror, Islamophobia, and (gay) rights discourses are *never* intertwined. Sometimes they are. But they are not *always* intertwined, as the Romania-EU example described above indicates.

Similarly, in "The Golden Handcuffs of Gay Rights: How Pinkwashing Distorts both LGBTIQ and Anti-Occupation Activism," Puar (2012) tells us that pinkwashing works for at least six main reasons. These include, among others, the historical endurance of The Woman Question (and now, presumably, The Homosexual Question); the global proliferation of Islamophobia engendered by the War on Terror (as well as forms of Islamophobia that pre-date September 11th); a proliferation of Euro-American constructs of identity, and so on and so forth. But, in the sixth reason she identifies, Puar proceeds to claim that pinkwashing "is to a large extent directed toward the United States, Israel's greatest financial supporter internationally, and more generally to Euro-American gays who have the political capital and financial resources to invest in Israel" (Puar 2012).

The suggestion here appears to be that the United States is complicit in Israeli pinkwashing and indeed underwrites it—a claim justified by the statement that the United States is Israel's greatest financial supporter. But the United States is a major financial supporter to many states, including, as it turns out, Palestine.[7] Equally, as of 2017, the top three recipients of US funding and weapons happened to be: Israel, Egypt, and Afghanistan (Najjar 2017).

To say, therefore, that the United States is the "greatest financial supporter" of any given country does not mean anything very significant at all. The full implication of Puar's reading of this context would suggest that US funding underwrites all of the following: The Israeli occupation, the Palestinian resistance to the Israeli occupation, homophobia in Egypt, sexism in Afghanistan, and so on and so forth. But this is undoubtedly not what Puar intends to say.

By selectively curating the information she divulges to her readers about the US's financial involvement in West Asia, Puar not only makes a series of misleading statements but also infantilizes her intended audience. Why does she insist on doing this? Well, my guess is: It is inconvenient for her to delineate the details of the US's financial involvement in the region because that would, in turn, cannibalize her ability to denounce the US's friendly ties with Israel—and Puar is clearly deeply committed to the latter.

This is what I mean by Radical Theory Creep. Puar lets her analysis of Israeli pinkwashing commit an overreach as she attempts to expand the ambit of this analysis to further encode within it a set of critiques that is wider than what the category was originally intended for. The result?

A critical loss of analytical and methodological rigor. Ian Shapiro identifies a version of this problem when he suggests: "if the only tool you have is a hammer, everything around you starts to look like a nail" (Shapiro 2002, 598).

And so it is that in "Rethinking Homonationalism" (2013) we are given such a dizzying range of semantic conflations that it is hard to remember, finally, what pinkwashing *actually is*. Here is a relevant excerpt:

> [P]inkwashing is one manifestation and practice made possible within and because of homonationalism. Unlike pinkwashing, homonationalism is not a state practice per se. It is instead the historical convergence of state practices, transnational circuits of queer commodity culture and human rights paradigms, and broader global phenomena such as the increasing entrenchment of Islamophobia....Pinkwashing works in part by tapping into the discursive and structure circuits produced by the U.S. and European crusades against the spectral threat of "radical Islam" or Islamo-fascism. (Puar 2013, 337–338)

Let's consider seriously what we have here. From this excerpt, we have come to learn that: (1) pinkwashing succeeds by relying upon discursive circuits which are themselves sustained by crusades against, *inter alia*, Islamo-fascism; (2) that pinkwashing is a manifestation of homonationalism; and (3) that homonationalism itself includes Islamophobia.

Ergo, pinkwashing is Islamophobic. But is this *always* true? What is going on here is a critique of a list of oppressions that is itself predicated on a convergence of concepts of disparate, radical, anti-imperialistic, anti-homophobic, anti-colonial, and anti-capitalistic ideas that are getting melded into one amorphous set of interrelated critiques of statecraft, war, diplomacy, international human rights discourses, commodity culture, capitalism, colonialism, racism, neoliberalism, Islamophobia, and (by extension, in many countries of the Global North) xenophobia. This cluster of concepts is then being called homonationalism.

But this is not an "ism." This is a shopping cart.

The jaw-dropping claim here is that *it is possible to have a singular theory* of resistance for this entire complicated network of violences. But this is not all. Puar also makes two ancillary claims about homonationalism.

First, we are told: "Like modernity, homonationalism can be resisted and re-signified, but not opted out of: we are all conditioned by it and through it" (Puar 2013, 336). This stipulation, of course, has a chilling effect on speech. One is stunned into silence. Are we really *all* conditioned by and through homonationalism? It *can't* be opted out of? So, then, is *everything* tinged by it? If so, how, then, are we also being told—and this is the second claim—that: "homonationalism is an analytic category deployed to understand and historicize how and why such a status ("gay-friendly") has become desirable in the first place" (Puar 2013, 336)?

Something is not right here. Homonationalism is being presented here as both an analytic category and the object of the analysis. In the resulting confusion, a number of questions present themselves: Who is doing the deployment? And who, after all, is doing the understanding and historicization? And why, if everyone is always already unable to opt out of homonationalism, are we to take seriously any one particular individual's deployment of this analytic category? Or, are we being told, implicitly, that some people are better able to "resist" homonationalism, and, *a fortiori*, in a more suitable (superior?) position to deploy such an analytical category? If so, how are we to know who these people are, and how, indeed, have they come to possess this invulnerability that has eluded so many of the rest of us?

The problems identified here appear, finally, to be the result of Puar's commitment to a totalizing critique. But the difficulty is that the interrelated critiques Puar is committed to offering cannot be easily bundled into one parsimonious framework without a major loss of analytical power. This is not to say that the convergences that homonationalism purports to identify do not exist. But, instead, it is to say that it cannot be given *one* name—as if it is always already *one* thing. These convergences are braided differently at different times, with variously unfolding, and self-rearranging, permutations and concatenations. Inasmuch as there is homonationalism, there are only homonationalisms. It takes one shape and form in one context and quite another in a different one. And each context-specific instantiation of homonationalism should be engaged with on its own, specific, terms. Homonationalism in the US context has a very different set of implications for the world, for example, than that emanating from, say, Argentina or Romania.

Unlike what Puar suggests, pinkwashing is not *always* a "manifestation" of homonationalism, if homonationalism is defined, as Puar elects to define it, as always already Islamophobic. To be perfectly sure, such an instance of pinkwashing *could very well be* one manifestation of homonationalism but it *does not have to be*. The two propositions are not the same and it behooves us to remain mindful of the distinction in no small part because these sweeping conflations and generalizations have pernicious consequences. (I address this claim in greater detail in Sect. 2.5.)

But, before that, here is an excerpt from Dean Spade, in which he reconfirms Puar's imagery of the imbricated nature of human rights violations, warfare, pinkwashing, US foreign policy, and Islamophobia:

> At the DNC and his inauguration, Obama's support for same-sex marriage similarly helped him portray his administration as progressive and equality loving in order to obscure his abysmal record on key issues such as austerity, his failure to close Guantanamo, ongoing drone strikes, harsh sanctions against Iran, the long wars in Iraq and Afghanistan, and his record-breaking rates of deportation. [Citation omitted here.] Purported support for "gay rights," regardless of whether those rights are recognized in the U.S. or if they actually prevent or reduce harm facing queer and trans people, is used as a rationale for domestic and international regimes of racialized violence and warfare that continue to expand under the Obama administration. These declarations of gay rights aim to distract from and justify—to pinkwash—the brutal realities of U.S. politics and policy. (Spade 2013, 87)

Spade suggests here, in the same breath, both that the Obama administration uses its "declarations of gay rights" to pinkwash and that its support for gay rights is "used as a rationale for domestic and international regimes of racialized violence and warfare." But, what is astonishing is that Spade does not feel it necessary to *demonstrate* it to be the case here that the Obama administration has used its support for gay rights as a way to *rationalize* the forms of violence it has visited upon people. Indeed, Spade's analysis presents us with the one-sided "ideological Möbius strip" (Edelman 2004, 2) referred to in Chapter 1. It matters, for the purposes of the point I am making here, not very much at all whether or not the Obama administration has, in fact, done this. What is important is that this is not something one ought to simply assert, by fiat, and not support with evidence. Why should we take Spade's word for granted on this issue? Is Spade insinuating that he knows something that we do not? If so, it behooves him to let us know *whence* he knows this.

Spade also thinks that the controversy surrounding the repeal of Don't Ask Don't Tell (DADT) in the United States was accompanied by "ubiquitous imagery of gay soldiers kissing in uniform, to obscure the current [at the time] realities of U.S. military imperialism."

Again, no evidence or citation is provided here to support the claim that this imagery was indeed ubiquitous in the United States. Instead, we are told, again, merely as an assertion, that "the loud drumbeat of anti-Muslim racism combines with the sentimental lovesongs of gay and lesbian military pride to drown out critiques of war and militarism." Spade is also silent about the uncomfortable reality that patriotic gays and lesbians have always, at least in one view, underwritten US imperialism by serving in the US military even under oppressive injunctions to convert or to pass. Indeed, it is their involvement with the military, and not their withdrawal, that has allowed the US military, in part, to bring the "'homosexual' into being" as a "social and legal subject" (Lehring 2003, 6).

According to Spade, Islamophobia is linked to the US's military adventures and a "pro-military sentiment" is linked to "anti-homophobia" (Spade 2013, 92–93). The result is that, in Spade's telling, these things are all presented as semantic cousins: Islamophobia, anti-homophobia, and pro-military sentiment. However, as proof for these claims, Spade offers only one concrete piece of evidence, or so he thinks. Thus, we come to learn that the 2009 Matthew Shepard, James Byrd Jr. Act was "a bill [that became law] that added "sexual orientation" and "gender identity or expression" to the federal hate crimes statute as an amendment to the Fiscal Year 2008 Department of Defense Authorization Bill"; it also "set aside the highest amount of money ever provided to the Department of Defense in U.S. history" (Spade 2013, 92). Spade then cites Chandan Reddy, who has claimed that it was an "act of genius" (Reddy, quoted in Spade [2013, 92]) on the part of Congressional Democrats to attach the hate crimes bill on to a defense spending bill which, in Spade's own words, "brought Republican support needed to pass the hate crime law" (Spade 2013, 93).

But if this is indeed what is going on here, then there is a word for it: "politics." Congressional Democrats are tacking on to a bill—that Republicans are sure to support—a pet cause of their own so that they can get around Republican obstructionism. Why *must* this be necessarily characterized as a "link" between anti-homophobia and pro-military sentiment? Who is establishing this link? For whose benefit? Who is anti-homophobic here and who is not? And who is pro-military here and who is not? Surely, we can't go along with Spade, if he is meaning to suggest that everyone here is pro-military and everyone here is anti-homophobic. The claim seems highly unlikely, if not entirely dubious. Not to mention, the proposition also begs proof.

In the same essay, Spade also calumniates Hillary Clinton's 2011 "Gay Rights Are Human Rights" speech at the United Nations: It is an act of pinkwashing, we are told, that is also closely affiliated with the "anti-Arab" and "anti-Muslim" trappings of the—(admittedly) stupefyingly irrational and inhumane—War on Terror. Thus, we are informed here that the United States "will now use gay rights to exert pressure on countries where the US has some ulterior motive" (Spade 2013, 93). But we are never told: (a) what these ulterior motives are; and (b) how Spade actually knows this to be the case. This is Radical Theory Creep hard at work. Everything happens quickly and all the key claims are shrouded in mystery. Before we even realize it, what begins as a statement about the speech's pinkwashing elements suddenly slips into the assertion that gay rights are being proffered as a justification here for "anti-Muslim framings" (Spade 2013, 87). It bears quoting this segment at some length here:

> Hilary Clinton's 2011 speech declaring that "gay rights are human rights," along with the prevalence of references to same-sex marriage and gay rights at the 2012 Democratic National Convention (DNC) and Obama's reference to gay marriage in his 2013 inauguration speech, are examples of American *pinkwashing*. Clinton's speech evinces a relatively new logic in U.S. imperialism: that the U.S., regardless of failures to protect queer and trans people from state violence at home, will now use gay rights to exert pressure on countries where the U.S. has some ulterior motive. Clinton uses lesbian and gay rights to bolster the notion that the U.S. is the world's policing arm, forcing democracy and equality globally on purportedly backward and cruel governments. Gay rights operates as a new justification for this imperial role—a justification that fits well within the *anti-Arab and anti-Muslim framings* that have been developed during the War on Terror and portray Arab and Muslim countries as more sexist and homophobic than the U.S., European countries and Israel. (Spade 2013, 87, emphasis mine)

What the reader comes away with from this is a false dichotomy. You either accept as evidence for the claims the very self-evident tone of the writing or you must be someone who refuses to accept that US pinkwashing and Islamophobia are (always) intertwined. And we all know what the latter means. (Everything takes the form, style, and content of academic tongue-in-cheek.) It means that you are unwilling to decry Islamophobia.

The problem here is that Spade does not engage at all with Clinton's own call—in this very same speech—to fight *against* Islamophobia.

In citing the important role of allies in dismantling any form of group oppression,[8] Clinton actually *analogizes* homophobia to Islamophobia and other forms of discrimination and explicitly calls upon us *all* to share in the responsibility to end it:

> In the fight for women's rights, the support of men remains crucial. The fight for racial equality has relied on contributions from people of all races. Combating *Islamaphobia* or anti-Semitism is a task for people of all faiths. And the same is true with this struggle for equality. (Clinton 2011, emphasis mine)

Such analogies, in fact, *permeate* the whole speech. Clinton invites us to think about what it would mean to "walk a mile in someone else's shoes" (Clinton 2011). She asks us to think about racial minorities, women, religious, tribal, or ethnic minorities, children, people with disabilities, immigrants, workers, and so on. She seems particularly invested in thinking about race. Thus, she reminds us that just like slavery was once thought to be sanctioned by God and is "now properly reviled as an unconscionable violation of human rights," we should remember that a practice, even if it is publicly justified as a religious or cultural value at any given time may, in fact, be wrong. Equally, she reminds her audience that in the United States when President Truman desegregated the military many thought he was making a grave error. She then points out that the action has led to a strengthening of "our social fabric in ways even the supporters of the policy could not foresee" (Clinton 2011).

Unfortunately, however, all of this escapes the attention of Anna Aganthangelou who, in her effort to "reengage with Hillary Clinton's UN speech" (Agathangelou 2013, 455), spectacularly misreads it and instead declares that: "Clinton separates sexual identity (as opposed to queerness) and slavery (as opposed to race)" (Agathangelou 2013, 457). This proposition is patently false because Clinton, as discussed above, does not, in fact, separate the question of "sexual identity"[9] and "slavery." The truth is that Clinton, contrary to what Agathangelou is claiming, *highlights* the interconnections between the two.

Agathangelou also appears to be confused about the complicated category of SOGI (sexual orientation and gender identity).[10] What, for example, does she mean by "sexual identity" in the above-quoted excerpt? Does she mean sexual orientation? Or gender identity? Or some combination of the two? Or does she mean a "gay/lesbian" identity?

And why does she claim that this identity is opposed to "queerness"? And who is opposing "sexual identity" to "queerness" here? Is Clinton doing this? Or is Agathangelou herself saying that these two things are, in fact, "opposed" to each other?

None of this is clear.

Consequently, the reader has no idea at all what Agathangelou means, except that we can all realize she is saying something vaguely hostile about Clinton's speech. Aganthangelou's Radical Theory Creep is perhaps the most egregious of all the examples I have engaged with so far in this chapter, as in, for example, when she claims—presumably as critique (?)—that in the speech Clinton "argues that the only way that certain nations can become democratic spaces is by eradicating violence against gays" (Agathangelou 2013, 456). There are at least two problems with this claim. First, it is not at all clear why it would be a bad thing in the world if violence against gays were to be eradicated. The second problem is that Clinton does not, in fact, make this argument, as Agathangelou so misleadingly suggests. There is no part of the text of the Clinton speech that can reasonably be read as advancing the proposition that *the only way* for certain nations to become democratic is by eradicating violence against gays. Agathangelou also claims, falsely, that:

> In Hillary Clinton's speech, we see a move to foist the imperative of a West [sic] gay homogeny internationally. In deploying US gay and lesbian relations at the level of world order [Clinton] universalizes what she thinks are sexual-state-capital revolutionizing relations. She proceeds to argue that those states that do not take seriously this revolutionizing of sexuality would not receive aid from the US. (Agathangelou 2013, 458)

Again, Clinton does not do this.[11] She never argues that those who do not fall in line with her anti-homophobic injunctions "would not receive aid from the US." The closest thing she says in the speech that might be read in this fashion is her one, solitary, utterance about "foreign assistance":

> Building on efforts already underway at the State Department and across the government, the President has directed all U.S. Government agencies engaged overseas to combat the criminalization of LGBT status and conduct, to enhance efforts to protect vulnerable LGBT refugees and asylum seekers, to ensure that our foreign assistance promotes the protection

> of LGBT rights, to enlist international organizations in the fight against discrimination, and to respond swiftly to abuses against LGBT persons. (Clinton 2011)

This is a classic move in Radical Theory Creep. A statement that says that the President has directed all US government agencies to ensure that "our foreign assistance promotes the protection of LGBT rights" is here being recast as a threat from Clinton that suggests that "those states that do not take [LGBT+ rights] seriously...would not receive aid from the US" (Agathangelou 2013, 458). This is not to say that the two propositions are radically dissimilar, but instead to stipulate—now and forever—that they are decisively not identical and should not be mischaracterized as such.

What I have tried to show so far is that Radical Theory Creep has a thriving career. But we should resist it. I say this not because I think the United States never pinkwashes. As I describe in the next section, it does. I also do not say this because I believe that pinkwashing is never Islamophobic. It can be. Instead, I say this because I think that pinkwashing is *not always* Islamophobic and *not always* mobilized in the service of neo- or any other kind of imperialism.

Preserving this distinction is important for a number of reasons, several of which I address in some detail in the concluding section of this chapter. But before that, I discuss, in Sect. 2.4, how pinkwashing is a complicated category that does service as well disservice to the cause of justice and gay rights in the world. In doing so, I focus on Hillary Clinton's 2011 gay rights are human rights speech. As I demonstrate here, this rhetoric is very definitely an instance of pinkwashing, and even what Lisa Duggan and others have called homonormativity (Duggan 2002). But we also have to be mindful about two things about this speech: (a) we must be attentive to what this speech might "do in the world"; and (b) no reasonable interpretation of this speech can lead to the inference that it is, in fact, Islamophobic.

2.4 Hillary Clinton's "Gay Rights Are Human Rights" Speech: What It Is and What It Is not[12]

Cynthia Weber has offered an excellent and nuanced discussion of Hillary Clinton's gay rights are universal human rights speech. I want to emphasize this idea of nuance here because Weber actually makes two interesting—and apparently discordant—moves.[13] On the one hand, she acknowledges the problematic nature of the speech. In doing so, she highlights the "homonormative and homo(inter)nationalist moves" illustrated by the speech (Weber 2016, 113). On the other hand, Weber also cautions against taking it as axiomatic that the speech is "*necessarily* (neo)imperial" (Weber 2016, 119, emphasis in the original). In fact, according to Weber, the terms Clinton uses do not exhaustively define what this call for gay rights as human rights might "do in the world" (Weber 2016, 119). As Weber describes it, some of the political power of rights discourses actually inheres in their ability to exceed the terms in which they are articulated (Weber 2016, 119). In addition, Weber wisely reminds us that we also ought to think about what it would mean for the United States *not* to call for gay rights as human rights (Weber 2016, 119). I take Weber's reading of the speech seriously, while arguing, as I have briefly done elsewhere (Ghosh 2016), that Clinton's speech is indeed an act of pinkwashing. But, as I also demonstrate in the remainder of this section, by this I do not mean to suggest that the speech is Islamophobic, or that it is delivered in order to advance a US-backed neo-imperialism.

It is well known that President Obama and the-then Secretary of State Hillary Clinton herself have apparently "evolved," and taken their time to do so, on the question of gay rights as human rights and changed their minds about whether gay people should have the right to marry. It is also well known that the United States itself had sodomy laws on the books in several states till as late as 2003—one of the few countries of the Global North that still had these kinds of laws on the books (to be fair, Clinton does acknowledge this).[14]

So, it is actually easy—but ultimately quite simplistic—to focus exclusively on what might seem like hypocrisy in the way in which the speech can be used to leverage a pinkwashing agenda against countries that do not give their LGBT+ population rights and protections, and those that do not try to assimilate their queers into becoming "good gays" (Warner 1999; Duggan 2002; Weber 2016; Ghosh 2016). The reality is that across the world LGBT+ people have celebrated this speech, circulated it on social media, talked to their friends and families about it, and so on. Therefore, it matters and it does not that Hillary Clinton's own position on marriage equality has taken quite a bit of time to evolve. What matters—and matters more significantly—is that LGBT+ people in many parts of the Global South are grateful to her for delivering this speech.

In fact, some of us were very deeply moved when we first saw it/heard it/heard of it. So, it is important that Weber cautions us to remain mindful about what this speech might "do in the world."

In opposing this speech, it is also easy for us to say, as Sara Ahmed does in another context, citing Gayatri Spivak, that "homophobia" can be mobilized in the form of "white queers saving brown queers from brown straights" (Spivak, quoted in Ahmed [2011, 126]). But everything gets more complicated if we were to try to square this utterance with Spivak's own cautionary insight that points out that rights are something "we cannot not want" (Spivak, quoted in Franke [2012a, 4]). It behooves us, then, to think about Hillary Clinton's call for gay rights as human rights with some care. What might this speech, in fact, "do in the world"?

Historically, international human rights norms have had a woeful track record in addressing LGBT+ rights. The UDHR, for example, opens by citing the inherent dignity of the equal and inalienable rights of all members of the human family. It mentions freedom of speech and freedom from fear and want. Article 2 mentions non-discrimination on the basis of race, sex, color, language, religion, political opinion, national origin, etc. But there is no mention of sexual orientation or gender identity, even though the document does mention other rights relating to the right of intimate association, such as the right to marriage and family, without stipulation of gender.

The International Bill of Human Rights also succumbs to arguments from member-states premised on national sovereignty and the issue of "cultural relativism" (Tharoor 1999; Franck 2001). Thus, some member countries maintain that the Universal Declaration of Human Rights is a Eurocentric document and that sometimes non-western cultural practices and values can, and do, run up against western understandings of human rights. However, given the nature of sovereignty, nation-states should not be pressured by the international community into changing their laws. Sodomy law, or laws proscribing homosexuality, are prototypical examples of such resistance. In 2016, at least 73 countries (and 37% of UN member-states) had laws criminalizing homosexuality (Nunez 2016). It is not surprising, therefore, that there has been hardly any mention at all of LGBT+ rights in international human rights law—at least until recently.[15]

So, when a powerful globally recognized icon such as Hillary Clinton signals to the LBGT+ population around the world that the international community stands with them in solidarity, that utterance does quite a lot in the world—even though it runs the risk of (strategically?[16]) essentializing the experience of all LGBT+ persons as the same, or at the very least, as similar. It gives hope, courage, and strength to nascent LGBT+ rights movements in some countries that they have an ally in the international community. It reconfirms and bolsters these vulnerable populations' argument that they are not asking for extra entitlements or special rights but that they are demanding the protection of their fundamental rights. It adds pressure on the states that do have sodomy laws to publicly justify the existence of these laws to their people and to the international community. At the same time, one also should not erase the fact that the speech itself is part of a larger discursive context that interweaves strains from homonationalism (Puar 2007, 2013), homonormativity (Duggan 2002; Puar 2006), and pinkwashing (Schulman 2011; Franke 2012a; Ghosh 2016) with international affairs.

In recent years, under the Obama administration and indeed in the speech itself, the United States has repeatedly characterized the figure of the LGBT individual as a gay-rights-holder (Weber 2016). In doing so, it has actively contributed to US pinkwashing. And so has the Clinton speech. This figure of the gay-rights-holding individual is always presented as an unencumbered, abstract, identity-less, Kantian, and by that logic Rawlsian, individual. But somehow, they also have some of the following characteristics: They are privatized and depoliticized, and flourish only in domesticity, consumption, and what might be called homonormativity—this is the "good gay." The characterization here is unmistakably heteronormative but with its own, somewhat peculiar, aesthetics. They may or may not be repronormative[17]; but they never transgress any boundaries of civilized and bourgeois decency. They love; they marry; they do not cheat on their partner; they never cruise the streets; they shop; they spend money; they vacation; and—and, this is very important—they are HIV negative (Ghosh 2016).

In other words, this gay-rights-holder is a universal(ized) figure precisely because they are normal in every possible way. They are the not-perverse LGBT person. That does not mean there are no "perverse" (Weber 2016) homosexuals. But we are not talking about them here. Or really anywhere. Any talk about these *other* gays falls outside the range of conversations permissible in the elevated and hallowed registers of human rights discourse.

Weber is keenly aware that Clinton never says the word "homosexual"—and exclusively uses the less pathological signifier, "LGBT." This LGBT individual has the "right to have rights" (as Arendt would say) (Weber 2016, 110) and should be accorded status and recognition as full citizens. And here is where Clinton's move to pinkwashing is made more or less explicit in the speech.

If you are a state that does not accord an identical basket of rights and immunities to straight citizens and the domesticated LGBT+-identified individual, then you are on the wrong side of history. What this implies is that there is only one right side of history and the United States, the EU, and Israel—because they give gays and lesbians rights—are both standing and evolving on that very nice side of history. Clinton, in fact, *literally* says this: "There is a phrase that people in the United States invoke when urging others to support human rights: 'Be on the right side of history.'"

It is also significant that the relationships these "good" states have crafted with their good, homonormative, gays are mutually beneficial. Here's how: the state accords these people rights. And they, in turn, protect the homeland. They do so by doing one or both of two things. First, they preserve domestic tranquility and normalcy by staying true to their consumerist credentials and by thus sustaining neoliberal markets (Ghosh 2016). They sometimes help the economy by becoming entrepreneurial gays (Puar 2006). They also often do their part for a reproductive, loving, national family by bearing and/or raising children (Zivi 2014). And although apparently docile, they are nonetheless patriots (Puar 2006; Franke 2012a). Thus—and this is the second very nice thing that they do—since the repeal of Don't Ask Don't Tell, they also openly serve in the military and, in doing so, they more performatively protect the nation from foreign aggression (Spade 2013, 90–93).

The tiresome punch line, then, as must be obvious to anyone, is: You are a good gay or a "perverse homosexual"; you are a nice gay-friendly state or a state that persecutes its homosexuals; you are either on the right side of history or on the wrong side. Binaries abound.

Obviously, Clinton's pinkwashing will not stand up to the slightest scrutiny. What, after all, does the Secretary of State mean by rights? What precise rights is she talking about that are meant to accrue to this gay-rights-holder? Marriage rights? Political rights? Economic rights? Social rights? Cultural rights? The rights to physical security and bodily integrity? The right to life? Without further clarification, or so it would appear, the word "rights" means very little. To be sure, Clinton does try to clarify what rights she is talking about—but in doing so, she raises more questions than she resolves.

This happens, for example, in the case when Clinton mentions that LGBT+-identified individuals have the right to be treated as "equals" under the law. But this is a very tricky proposition. If, as we know, there are sodomy laws in place in 73+ countries (Nunez 2016), what specifically are the rights that are being withheld from the LGBT+ population that, by insinuation, the straight-identified/straight-performing population possesses? In many of these cases, laws that criminalize actions committed against the "order of nature," presumably apply equally to heterosexual and non-heterosexual people. In these legal regimes, even the act of heterosexual fellatio wouldn't pass constitutional muster—at least in theory. So, then, is "equality" violated by these sodomy laws? In her concurring opinion in *Lawrence v. Texas* (O'Connor 2003, 4), Justice Sandra Day O'Connor is concerned with exactly this issue when she declared that she found Texas's sodomy law to be unconstitutional because it violated the equal protection clause of the Fourteenth Amendment. This was because the law, as it was written, criminalized homosexual but not heterosexual sodomy.

More importantly, Clinton is calling out here for an equal right to do what, precisely? Choose intimate partners? But if that is a "human right," then most countries in the world curtail this right to some extent. All have, or have had, some restrictions on the range of people one can permissibly be sexually intimate with. Examples include categories like children, people with cognitive disabilities, family members, members of the same sex, the incarcerated, various racial minorities, various caste groups, and so on.

Clearly, then, which groups of individuals one may be disbarred from having sex with within a given context has historically depended on the cultural, social, religious, and political milieu and, above all, the law of a given land. In other words, these proscriptions have always been an artifact of that pole star of international relations: sovereignty. Why should LGBT+ people be an exception to this general practice? On what grounds? Clinton never explains.

At other points, Clinton mentions physical security and the right to have bodily integrity and freedom from violence, intimidation, and bullying. But if these are some of the rights she has in mind, she can't possibly be pinkwashing in the sense that she is presenting the United States as a place where these things do not happen. This is so because, as is well known, homophobic and trans*-phobic assault happens almost everywhere—in Chechnya, for example, but in the United States as well, as Clinton acknowledges.

Clinton also could not possibly be talking here about the "right" to marry. This is so because when she delivered the speech, the United States itself didn't have marriage equality. She does, however, mention the right to equal dignity. But she could not have been totally serious about this because the right to "equal dignity" is not something that US Courts recognized till 2015—well after the Clinton speech.[18] (It is even possible that Clinton's address not only foreshadowed but also influenced this development.)

Finally, Clinton does indeed talk specifically about the right to life. She condemns both judicial and extrajudicial (she mentions honor killings) executions of LGBT+ people. But extrajudicial murders of LGBT+ people happen in the United States all the time. *The L.A. Times*, for example, reported in November 2017 that at least 25 transgender people had been killed in the United States in 2017 alone—the "highest annual total on record" (Associated Press/L.A. Times 2017). But, in the discussion on state-endorsed executions, we might have at last found something concrete. Clinton might—just might—be talking about the right of LGBT+ persons to freedom from "judicial" killings. The United States—at the very least we can say—does not endorse this sort of thing. This finally gives her something to pinkwash with. But if all Clinton has in her arsenal to present gay rights as human rights is her belief in the freedom from state-sanctioned execution, then this is surely a tenuous theoretical hook on which she is trying to hang a very bold set of claims.

By presenting "rights" as a settled concept within a presumed (but eternally unspecified) linguistic community, therefore, Clinton elides a discussion of the *substantive* ways in which an entire gamut of rights violations is routinely experienced by sexual orientation, gender identity, and gender expression minorities both in the United States and elsewhere. These violations range from physical assault/murder to unequal pay to employment discrimination to simple disrespect and misrecognition. This stuff, quite simply, happens everywhere.

While it ought to be clear by now, from what I have said above, that I could not agree more with Weber that we need to remain mindful of what a statement like Clinton's might "do in the world," we might also want to acknowledge, with Weber, that the speech is eternally problematic. But here, below, is a description of what the speech is not:

It is not a dissertation in the field of analytic philosophy or logic. (It is, instead, a rhetorical and even political move. Clinton's call for "rights" here functions as a metonymic stand-in for a call for the eradication of homophobia.) And no reasonable or ordinary interpretation of the speech can lead to the conclusion that the speech is Islamophobic or homonationalist (if the latter is defined as anti-Muslim). It is a call to shame countries for not granting their LGBT+ individuals legal protections against discrimination and violence. It is an instance of the political pressure of pinkwashing being applied, just as the EU applied it in the case of Romania.

2.5 The Sad Case of Antinormative-Versus-Normative Binary Logics

Clinton's choices in this speech are both extremely familiar and utterly unenviable. She is trying to articulate a defense of LGBT+ rights while asking sovereign nation-states with homophobic statutes on the books to change their laws. Thus, she realizes even as she delivers the speech that she is banging her head against the wall of cultural relativism.[19] If you side with the sovereign right of nation-states to make their own laws, then you have to endorse proscriptions on homosexuality in the name of tolerance and cultural difference. If, on the other hand, you choose to affirm that LGBT+ persons have the right to protection from persecution and discrimination, you run the risk of being labeled Eurocentric, universalizing, reductionist, and imperial.

In Jenny Sharpe's (1993) telling, a version of this conundrum is faced by the reader of E.M. Forster's *A Passage to India*—a text in which Forster coerces the reader into the unenviable position of having to either side with Adela Quested, a white woman (in which case, we live with the specter of our own orientalism/racism), or with Dr. Aziz, a colonized man (in which case, we have to live with the specter of our own sexism and misogyny). Each choice makes us complicit in the oppression of the character we did not pick. In other words, we can't win. A liberal feminist engagement with this dilemma also appears in Susan Moller Okin's "Feminism and Multiculturalism: Some Tensions" (Okin 1998), in which Okin calls for a rejection of a docile tolerance of patriarchy in the name of multiculturalism. Clinton's intervention, therefore, represents a drop in an ocean of dilemmas regarding multiculturalism. Clinton, like the reader of *A Passage to India*, cannot win.

More specifically, in the context of pinkwashing that I have been addressing throughout this chapter, the difficulties present themselves in very clear form. On the one hand, we know that there are such things as predatory neoliberalism, the Israeli occupation, pinkwashing, Islamophobia, raw nationalism, tribal power struggles, and religious and ethnocentric fanaticism. We also know that these things, and others, are sometimes mobilized—in various combinations—in the service of political strategies. On the other hand, we also know that the LGBT+ populations in many countries live in the throes of a constant vulnerability. This is particularly true of many Arab and Muslim-majority areas of the world. For some of these individuals, an international consensus that gay rights are human rights might indeed go a long way, even when, and if, they see it as Eurocentric.

This is a cautionary insight for queer theorists of all kinds. We need to remain mindful that the anti-pinkwashing critique is not obligated to deny that sexual minorities struggle in some countries, many of which are Arab or Muslim-majority countries. As Franke has suggested, the real problem here is not that Islam is an "inherently (or particularly) 'homophobic' religion," (Franke 2012a, 45) but instead that some emergent strains of Islamism create the conditions of possibility for an extreme form of homophobia to thrive.

To acknowledge this does not make us Islamophobic. It makes us clear-headed. It is also alright for us to acknowledge that the particularity of calls for human rights, like those made by Clinton, "inevitably complicates a 'for or against' position on 'gay rights'" (Weber 2016, 118–119). The complexity of the real world thus gives the lie to the elaborately moralistic positions we can sometimes find ourselves trumpeting.

In the context of pinkwashing, Franke has also written about the "imperialism" (Franke 2012a, 34; also see Agathangelou and Ling 2009, especially Chapter 1) of binaries. Thus, any critique of Israeli state policy can get "immediately tagged as anti-Semitic" which can result in the "chilling effect of blowback" (Franke 2012a, 44). But this anxiety of being falsely accused of a stigmatized politics is experienced not only by those, like Franke, who mobilize a critique of pinkwashing, but also by those who critique the critiques of pinkwashing. If one critiques, as I have done here in this essay, some forms of the radical critique of pinkwashing, one runs an equal risk of being falsely accused of Islamophobia, neoliberalism, and homonationalism.

The impending threat of these arbitrary accusations is Radical Theory Creep's most insidious consequence, and one that poses the risk of alienating our allies. It misrecognizes the fact that some members of the dominant mainstream are in fact fighting with us and for our cause—and are being sincere when they declare their solidarity with us. Allies have, after all, always played a notable role in the fight for justice for marginalized people everywhere.

One powerful voice speaking at the Seneca Falls Convention (1848), one of the first meetings organized to rally support for the women's suffrage movement in the United States, was that of Frederick Douglass's. John Stuart Mill's "pro-feminist" 1869 essay entitled "The Subjection of Women" (Mill 1991 [1869]) remains a canonical argument for equality between the sexes and a strenuous and early critique of patriarchy, replete with calls for women's suffrage on utilitarian grounds. Even before that, the issue of slavery in the United States would never have culminated in the moral and armed struggle of the Civil War without the continuing and relentless support of (mainly northern) white abolitionists. White liberal participation in the black civil rights movement of the mid-60s in the United States was a significant impetus in the movement's success. Straight parents and family members of gays and lesbians routinely join pride marches, organize, and rally support for the rights of LGBT+ people—as do a range of other straight allies. Equally, native-born citizens in the United States have always made vociferous calls for the humane treatment of immigrants—authorized and unauthorized, children and adults, men and women, and skilled workers as well as unskilled workers. When Senator Tom Harkin introduced the bill on the Senate floor that would eventually become the Americans with Disabilities Act (1990), he delivered part of the speech in sign language for the benefit of his deaf brother. It turns out, all powerless minorities depend on their allies for support and solidarity as they make their demands for justice.

When apparently radical theorists accuse someone like Hillary Clinton of advancing, in the name of gay rights, a US-backed neo-imperialism that is always already intertwined with the US-led Global War on Terror, they produce an atmosphere of anxiety about gay rights. This is the sort of anxiety that is likely to make our allies pause and wonder, before they articulate any pro-gay rights stance, whether they will be able to publicly defend it when confronted with Radical Theory Creep.

Radical Theory Creep also has political consequences, especially in the United States, where liberals of all hues are increasingly under attack from mainstream conservatives as well as from the Alt Right. Elsewhere, I have argued that Hillary Clinton's defeat in the 2016 presidential elections was the result of not just one thing but different things happening in different parts of the country ("Panel Discussion: The 2016 Election: What Happened and Why?" 2016). The one thing that was uniform throughout the blue and purple states she lost, however, was the fact that parts of her base refused to come out and vote for her in these places. They did so in crucial part because of the canard that she is a wolf in sheep's clothing. Thus, we are repeatedly told that Clinton obstructs justice, she is corrupt, she was responsible for the Benghazi attacks, and—as I have described above—that her gay rights talk is nothing but a veneer for her Islamophobic support of imperialism. This is not to say that those who are critical of Clinton should have fallen in line with mainstream liberals and voted for her or to say that they have no right to criticize her. But, instead, it is to say that their critiques should correspond to reality and not be deployed as a politicized witch hunt as Radical Theory Creep invariably tends to become.

If we are wholeheartedly committed to justice for LGBT+ people, we have an obligation to resist Radical Theory Creep, the binary logics it produces, and insist, instead, with Aeyal Gross, that not all depictions of gay rights in Israel constitute propaganda (Franke 2012a, 43). And, by the same token, we should applaud some Israeli and Palestinian queer activists' and citizens' steadfast refusal to privilege either the homonormative good gays or a raw form of nationalism (Franke 2012a; Schotten and Maikey 2012). We must ask ourselves, as Cynthia Weber does, what might a speech like Clinton's "do in the world"? We should have the courage to defend our ability to critique an instance of pinkwashing even as we refuse, if we genuinely believe it to be the case, to say that it is an act of neo-imperialism or Islamophobia.

The hopeful news is that there is a way out of the dilemmas I have identified here. But that path is paved with humility. We should start by acknowledging that many of us are socialized into finding Manichean dramas appealing. Having a clear idea of what one is for and what one is against gives us a certain kind of clarity, and a sense of security, to articulate our thoughts, to express ourselves. It is extremely hard, on the other hand, to reconcile oneself to the fact that sometimes there is an unambiguous for/against position to be had and—at other times—there simply isn't such a position to be had. What ultimately matters is that we do not lose sight of the critical commitments that bring us to a question in the first place, and to know and observe that the task of queer/radical theory is an ongoing one, and it is to constantly interrogate the ontologies that are imposed upon us—regardless of whether these impositions are administered by others or if we impose them upon ourselves.

Notes

1. This is typically, but not always, conducted by the state. Non-state actors can pinkwash too. See, for example, Katherine Franke's discussion of Mahmoud Ahmadinejad's appearance at Columbia University in 2007, where a non-state actor like Columbia University President Lee Bollinger is described as pinkwashing as he highlights "the mistreatment of women and homosexuals in Iran" (Franke 2012a, 20).
2. I derive the term, of course, from "mission creep"—a phrase that denotes the (sometimes inexorable) expansion of a military mission. See, for example, Cushman (1993). It is very important that we give this phenomenon a specific name. Critical legal theorists have long pointed out that when there is no word for a specific form of oppression in a given cultural setting, it can be disabling in that we cannot identify them and express precisely what is going on. See, for example, the discussion on "Structural Determinism" in Delgado and Stefancic (2001). A case study of this problem appears in Morris et al. (2008).
3. I use the phrase "gay rights" interchangeably with LGBT+ rights.
4. The Obama administration is declared, for example, by Dean Spade, as using its pro-gay rights rhetoric to obscure its "abysmal record" (Spade 2013, 87) on other issues.
5. The word "pinkwashing" has at least two different meanings/usages. It is used to critique the marketing technique that commodifies the "cause" of breast cancer, as in when corporations "cynically [embrace] the pink ribbon campaign for breast cancer awareness" to promote their images (see, e.g., Weber [2016, 213, 7n]). In recent years, however, some LGBT+ rights activists, often radical-queer critics, have identified a specific phenomenon as "pinkwashing." In this usage, pinkwashing occurs when one—typically a state, but sometimes even a non-state actor—characterizes western or western-affiliated democracies of the Global North as havens of individual and human rights because they are, ostensibly, progressive, or can be depicted as such, on the question of LGBT+ rights, while demonizing, in the process, as grotesque human rights abusers,

those countries (often Muslim countries) that have fewer LGBT+ rights protections (Gross 2010; Schulman 2011; Franke 2012a; Spade 2013; Weber 2016; Puar and Mikdashi 2012a, b; Puar 2012, 2013). In the remainder of this chapter, I will be using the word in this latter sense.

6. Franke recognizes the irony in the phrase.
7. We know, for example, the United States is the biggest contributor of funds to both the UNHCR—the UN Refugee Agency (UNHCR) as well as the United Nations Relief and Works Agency for Palestine Refugees in the Near East (UNRWA). The UNRWA has the mandate of providing relief and human development to Palestinian refugees in Jordan, Lebanon, Syria, the Gaza Strip, and the West Bank, including East Jerusalem (UNRWA, "The United Nations and Palestinian Refugees," n.d., 4). Palestinian refugees outside of these areas receive aid and assistance from the UNHCR (UNRWA, "The United Nations and Palestinian Refugees," n.d., 11–12). As of the end of 2010, there were close to 4.9 million refugees registered with UNRWA (UNRWA, "In Figures," n.d.). As of 2017, the United States was the largest donor to the UNHCR, with a contribution of about $1.4 billion. The next biggest donor was the European Union, with a combined total of a little over $400 million (UNHCR, n.d.). The story is the same with the UNRWA (UNRWA, "2016 Pledges to UNRWA Programmes," n.d.; also see Estrin 2018). In January 2018, as news broke that the Trump administration was considering cutting off aid to UN agencies aiding Palestine, *National Public Radio* reported that behind-the-scenes Israel is nervous about such threats because it does not want a humanitarian disaster in its backyard. So, Israel actually supports—yes, supports—US aid to Palestine (Estrin 2018). This is not because the state of Israel has a humane attitude toward Palestinians. It does not. It is because it does not want to live with the consequences of the United States withdrawing this aid.
8. On the concept of oppression experienced by social groups *qua* groups, see the excellent discussions in Young (1990) and Fraser (1995, 1997).
9. This phrase is eternally problematic. More on this below.
10. On SOGI, see, for example, ARC International (2015).
11. The full, approximately 3750-word long, transcript of the speech appears in the Appendix.
12. Parts of the discussion presented here also appear elsewhere (see Ghosh 2016).
13. In a provocatively titled essay, "Fuck Nuance," Healy (2017) takes issue with a particular way of "adding complexity" to an existing sociological theory by introducing an "additional dimension, level, or aspect" to it (Healy 2017, 118–119). This is not what I mean by nuance here. Instead, I mean the word *literally*.

14. The United States finally eradicated all sodomy laws across the country in 2003. See *Lawrence v. Texas* (2003).
15. A complete list of SOGI statements issuing from the UN is available at ARC International (2015).
16. On "strategic essentialism," see Ashcroft et al. (2013, 96–98).
17. I engage with this concept in greater detail in Chapter 3.
18. The Court does so in *Obergefell v. Hodges* (2015). See, for example, Tribe (2015) and Yoshino (2015).
19. This is not to say that there is no such thing as cultural relativism. There is. But not everything that gets characterized as such needs to be taken at face value. See, for example, Tharoor (1999/2000) and Franck (2001).

References

Agathangelou, Anna, and L.H.M. Ling. 2009. *Transforming World Politics: From Empire to Multiple Worlds.* New York: Routledge.

Agathangelou, Anna. 2013. "Neoliberal Geopolitical Order and Value: Queerness as a Speculative Economy and Anti-Blackness as Terror." *International Feminist Journal of Politics* 15 (4): 453–476.

Ahmed, Sara. 2011. "Problematic Proximities: Or Why Critiques of Gay Imperialism Matter." *Feminist Legal Studies* 19: 119–132.

ARC International. 2015. "SOGI Statements." ARC International (2015): SOGI Statements. http://arc-international.net/global-advocacy/sogi-statements/.

Ashcroft, Bill, Gareth Griffiths, and Helen Tiffin. 2013. *Postcolonial Studies: The Key Concepts*, 3rd ed. New York: Routledge.

Associated Press/L.A. Times. 2017. "Transgender People Are Being Killed at a Record Pace in U.S., Advocacy Groups Say." *L.A. Times*, November 17. http://www.latimes.com/nation/nationnow/la-na-transgender-homicides-20171117-story.html.

Clinton, Hillary. 2011. "Hillary Clinton on Gay Rights Abroad: Secretary of State Delivers Historic LGBT Speech in Geneva (Video, Full Text)," December 6. https://www.huffingtonpost.com/2011/12/06/hillary-clinton-gay-rights-speech-geneva_n_1132392.html.

Cushman, John H. 1993. "Mission in Somalia Is to Secure City." *The New York Times*, October 10. http://www.nytimes.com/1993/10/10/world/mission-in-somalia-is-to-secure-city.html?pagewanted=print&src=pm.

Delgado, Richard, and Jean Stefancic. 2001. *Critical Race Theory: An Introduction.* New York: New York University Press.

Duggan, Lisa. 2002. "The New Homonormativity: The Sexual Politics of Neoliberalism." In *Materializing Democracy: Toward a Revitalized Cultural*

Politics, edited by Russ Castronovo and Dana Nelson, 175–194. Durham, NC: Duke University Press.

Edelman, Lee. 2004. *No Future: Queer Theory and the Death Drive*. Durham, NC: Duke University Press.

Estrin, Daniel. 2018. "Trump Threatens to Withhold Aid to Palestinians." *National Public Radio*, January 3.

Franck, Thomas. 2001. "Are Human Rights Universal?" *Foreign Affairs*, January/ February. https://www.foreignaffairs.com/articles/afghanistan/2001-01-01/ are-human-rights-universal.

Franke, Katherine. 2012a. "Dating the State: The Moral Hazards of Winning Gay Rights." *Columbia Human Rights Law Review* 44 (1): 1–46.

———. 2012b. "The Greater Context of the Pinkwashing Debate." *Tikkun*, July 3. http://www.tikkun.org/nextgen/the-greater-context-of-the-pinkwashing-debate.

Fraser, Nancy. 1995. "From Redistribution to Recognition: Dilemmas of Justice in a 'Postsocialist' Age." *New Left Review* 1/212 (July–August): 68–93.

———. 1997. *Justice Interruptus: Critical Reflections on the "Postsocialist" Condition*. New York: Routledge.

Ghosh, Cyril. 2016. "Queer International Relations (1v): Queer as Method." *The Disorder of Things* (Blog), November 24. https://thedisorderofthings. com/2016/11/24/queer-international-relations-iv-queer-as-method/.

Gross, Aeyal. 2010. "Israeli GLBT Politics Between Queerness and Homonationalism." *Bully Bloggers*, July 3. https://bullybloggers.wordpress. com/2010/07/03/israeli-glbt-politics-between-queerness-and-homonationalism/.

Healy, Kieran. 2017. "Fuck Nuance." *Sociological Theory* 35 (2): 118–127.

Lehring, Gary. 2003. *Officially Gay: The Political Construction of Sexuality*. Philadelphia: Temple University Press.

Mill, John Stuart. 1991. *On Liberty and the Subjection of Women*, edited by *John Gray*. Oxford: Oxford University Press.

Morris, Wendy L., Bella M. DePaulo, Janina Hertel, and Lindsay C. Taylor. 2008. "Singlism-Another Problem That Has No Name: Prejudice, Stereotypes and Discrimination Against Singles." In *The Psychology of Modern Prejudice*, edited by Melanie A. Morrison and Todd G. Morrison, 165–194. Hauppauge, NY: Nova Science Publishers.

Najjar, Farah. 2017. "Why US Aid to Egypt Is Never Under Threat." *Al Jazeera*, October 3. http://www.aljazeera.com/news/2017/10/aid-egypt-threat-171002093316209.html.

Nunez, Christina. 2016. "Map Shows Where Being LGBT Can Be Punishable by Law." *National Geographic*, June 16. http://news.nationalgeographic. com/2016/06/lgbt-laws-gay-rights-world-map.

O'Connor, Sandra Day. 2003. *Lawrence v. Texas*.

Okin, Susan Moller. 1998. "Feminism and Multiculturalism: Some Tensions." *Ethics* 108 (4), 661–684.

"Panel Discussion: The 2016 Election: What Happened and Why?" 2016. https://www.youtube.com/watch?v=u9wAFScc2ww.

Puar, Jasbir. 2006. "Mapping US Homonormativities: Gender, Place and Culture: A Journal of Feminist Geography" 13 (1): 67–88.

———. 2007. *Terrorist Assemblages: Homonationalism in Queer Times*. Durham, NC: Duke University Press.

———. 2010. "To Be Gay and Racist Is No Anomaly." *Guardian*, June 2. http://www.theguardian.com/commentisfree/2010/jun/02/gay-lesbian-islamophobia.

———. 2012. "The Golden Handcuffs of Gay Rights: How Pinkwashing Distorts Both LGBTIQ and Anti-Occupation Activism." *The Feminist Wire*, January 30. http://www.thefeministwire.com/2012/01/the-golden-handcuffs-of-gay-rights-how-pinkwashing-distorts-both-lgbtiq-and-anti-occupation-activism/.

———. 2013. "Rethinking Homonationalism." *International Journal of Middle East Studies* 45: 336–339.

Puar, Jasbir, and Maya Mikdashi. 2012a. "Pinkwatching and Pinkwashing: Interpenetration and Its Discontents." *Jadaliyya*, August 9. http://www.jadaliyya.com/pages/index/6774/pinkwatching-and-pinkwashing_interpenetration-and.

———. 2012b. "On Positionality and Not Naming Names: A Rejoinder to the Response by Maikey and Schotten," October 10. http://Www.Jadaliyya.Com/Pages/Index/7792/On-Positionality-and-Not-Naming-Names-A-Rejoinder-to-the-Response-by-Maikey-and-Schotten.

Schotten, Heike, and Haneen Maikey. 2012. "Queers Resisting Zionism: On Authority and Accountability Beyond Homonationalism." *Jadaliyya*, October 10. http://www.jadaliyya.com/Details/27175/Queers-Resisting-Zionism-On-Authority-and-Accountability-Beyond-Homonationalism.

Schulman, Sarah. 2011. "Israel and 'Pinkwashing.'" *The New York Times*, November 22. http://www.nytimes.com/2011/11/23/opinion/pinkwashing-and-israels-use-of-gays-as-a-messaging-tool.html.

Shapiro, Ian. 2002. "Problems, Methods, and Theories in the Study of Politics, or What's Wrong with Political Science and What to Do about It." *Political Theory* 30 (4): 596–619.

Sharpe, Jenny. 1993. "The Unspeakable Limits of Civility: A Passage to India." In *Allegories of Empire: The Figure of Woman in the Colonial Text*, edited by Jenny Sharpe. Minneapolis, MN: University of Minnesota Press.

Spade, Dean. 2013. "Under the Cover of Gay Rights." *NYU Review of Law and Social Change* 37: 79–100.

Surasky, Cecilie. 2009. "Naomi Klein Shows You Can Boycott Israel Without Cutting Off Dialogue Over Palestine." *AlterNet*, August 31. https://www.alternet.org/story/142341/naomi_klein_shows_you_can_boycott_israel_without_cutting_off_dialogue_over_palestine.

Tharoor, Shashi. 1999. "Are Human Rights Universal?" *World Policy Journal* 16 (4): 1–6. http://www.worldpolicy.org/tharoor.html.

Tribe, Laurence. 2015. "Equal Dignity: Speaking Its Name." *Harvard Law Review* 129: 16–32.

UNHCR. n.d. "Donors." http://www.unhcr.org/en-us/donors.html.

UNRWA. n.d. "2016 Pledges to UNRWA's Programmes (Cash and In-Kind)—Overall Donor Ranking as 31 December 2016." https://www.unrwa.org/sites/default/files/donor_ranking_with_un_agencies_overall.pdf.

———. n.d. "In Figures: As of 30 December 2010." https://www.unrwa.org/userfiles/2011080123958.pdf.

———. n.d. "The United Nations and Palestinian Refugees." https://www.unrwa.org/userfiles/2010011791015.pdf.

Warner, Michael. 1999. *The Trouble with Normal: Sex, Politics and the Ethics of Queer Life*, 2nd ed. New York: Free Press.

Weber, Cynthia. 2016. *Queer International Relations: Sovereignty, Sexuality and the Will to Knowledge*. New York: Oxford University Press.

Yoshino, Kenji. 2015. "The Supreme Court, 2014 Term–Comment: A New Birth of Freedom?" *Harvard Law Review* 129: 77–85.

Young, Iris Marion. 1990. *Justice and the Politics of Difference*. Princeton, NJ: Princeton University Press.

Zivi, Karen. 2014. "Performing the Nation: Contesting Same-Sex Marriage Rights in the United States." *Journal of Human Rights* 13 (September): 290–306.

CHAPTER 3

Obergefell v. Hodges: Marriage Equality's Insistence on Family Values

Abstract In this chapter, I critically analyze the legal reasoning that undergirds the US Supreme Court's majority opinion in *Obergefell v. Hodges* (2015), a judgment that made marriage equality the law of the land in all 50 states. In so doing, I draw upon some insights from queer theorists, who point out the dangers of "normifying" any particular way of life because it marginalizes those who will not, or cannot, assimilate into the dominant culture. Here, I analyze the assimilationist tropes of amatonormativity and repronormativity that appear in the opinion in order to point out that these rhetorical tropes alienate everybody except the most conformist of gays and lesbians. The Court's reasoning is invested in LGBT+ normalization and endorses one particular conception of the good intimate life. Instead of this, the decision, I suggest, should have followed an approach steeped in what Cass Sunstein has called "decisional minimalism." Following such an approach would have enhanced, rather than constricted, the range of family formations endorsed by the state in *Obergefell*.

Keywords Amatonormativity · Decisional minimalism
Homonormativity · Marriage equality · *Obergefell v. Hodges*
Repronormativity

C. Ghosh, *De-Moralizing Gay Rights*,
https://doi.org/10.1007/978-3-319-78840-1_3

3.1 Introduction

Two US Supreme Court decisions have together established marriage equality in the United States. The first is *United States v. Windsor* (2013; hereafter, *Windsor*), which made it possible for same-sex marriage contracts to be recognized as such by the federal government. This federal recognition of same-sex marriage did not, however, resolve the dispute surrounding marriage equality in the United States once and for all. In the aftermath of *Windsor* (2013), several states continued to deny marriage licenses to same-sex couples and some did not recognize marriages performed in states where same-sex marriage was permissible. As a result of the discrepancy, and "circuit split" (Ford 2014), stemming from the recognition of same-sex marriage by the federal government and some states but not others, a spate of lawsuits ensued. In 2014, one set of cases—consolidated as *Obergefell v. Hodges* (2015; hereafter, *Obergefell*)—was granted certiorari by the Supreme Court. The Court's opinion in *Obergefell*, written by Justice Anthony Kennedy, finally struck down all statewide bans on same-sex marriage in the United States.

The Court's legal reasoning in *Obergefell*, however, has been widely criticized. These critiques are usually offered as one or the other, or some combination of, two species of criticisms. The first posits that the reasoning is shallow and predicated in large part on rhetorical flourishes rather than tightly logical argumentation. Ilya Somin has called the opinion "far from satisfying" because of its "dubious reasoning" (Somin 2015). Writing for *Slate*, Mark Joseph Stern suggests that the decision is "stuffed with sweetly teary-eyed turns of phrase" (Stern 2015).

The second species of critique tracks a familiar divide between legal scholars on the question of constitutional interpretation and points out that the reasoning furnishes no justification for its apparent discovery of a novel constitutional right—the right to equal dignity—that is, to be perfectly sure, nowhere explicitly enshrined in the Constitution. In this view, the decision is arbitrary and an instance of extreme judicial activism. Thus, Augusto Zimmerman (2015) has made the case that the Court's opinion is an instance of "arbitrary control." According to Alan Brownstein, the decision also raises concerns about government interference, especially in the area of religious liberty (2015).

Elsewhere, I have offered a textual exegesis of the opinion and pointed out that the decision advances a specific conception of the good that proposes an ideal to which all people, including homophobic critics of same-sex marriage as well as radical critics of *all* marriage, must assimilate (Ghosh 2018). In this chapter, I revisit this critique of assimilation but with a different objective. Here, I consider seriously what a non-assimilationist form of legal reasoning that the Court could have relied upon in *Obergefell* would look like. As I argue at greater length below, a decision in *Obergefell* that refrained from any endorsement of a particular conception of the good would have abided by what Cass Sunstein has called an approach rooted in "decisional minimalism" (Sunstein 1996, 1999). Minimalist decisions represent a commitment to both narrowness and shallowness. They are restrained and incremental and appear as if one is not aggressively taking sides in a polarizing conflict. Consequently, minimalist decisions reduce any suspicions about the Court's own partisanship, especially among losing litigants which, in turn, has the effect of tempering, rather than exacerbating, the conflict at hand.

The legal reasoning offered in *Obergefell* is the very opposite of minimalist. In fact, it aggressively advances a very particular conception of the good. Two characteristics of the decision are examined here closely to illustrate this point in detail: amatonormativity and repronormativity.[1] The former attaches special value to the amorous and romantic dyad, while the latter privileges the nuclear family, parenting, and, in some cases, even the begetting of children. In so doing, both mobilize certain dimensions of heteronormativity even as they eschew heteronormativity's central injunction to preserve traditional gender roles. In relying on these amatonormative and repronormative traditions to structure a legal opinion, the *Obergefell* decision positions itself as speaking on behalf of a state that has a very clear and specific conception of the "good" intimate life. The opinion signals the extent to which the state *wants* marriage, monogamy, parenting, and the nuclear family to be the norm for all—as well as the Court's abiding commitment to LGBT+ assimilation into mainstream American society.

In Sect. 3.2, I begin by delineating a queer critique of the kinds of assimilationist injunctions we find in *Obergefell*. As indicated above, here I focus on two tropes within the text of the opinion that are particularly oppressive for those who do not or cannot assimilate into Justice Kennedy's vision of the good life: amatonormativity and repronormativity. In Sect. 3.3, I point out how an approach based on decisional minimalism would have enabled the Court to issue an opinion that would have eschewed both amatonormative and repronormative injunctions. As a result, I suggest, the judgment would be more firmly committed to expanding, rather than constricting, the emancipatory goal of allowing a diverse range of family formations to thrive in the United States.

3.2 The Queer Preference for Non-endorsement[2]

The assimilationist injunctions in *Obergefell* inhere in the opinion's signaling that the justification for marriage equality is grounded in two central elements of traditional family life. The first is the figure of the dyadic romantic couple and the second consists of difficulties associated with bringing up children in households headed by two parents who are not married to each other. Both of these concerns are rejected by queer theorists who have historically resisted discursive formations that advance the claim that there is only one, particular, good way to form a family or indeed to live out intimacies.

Thus, radical/queer theorists identify a distinction between normals—mainstream gays and lesbians who want to assimilate into the rest of society—and queers, who reject any demand for assimilation and identify closely with the "difference" that has historically been ascribed to them (see Warner 1999; Yoshino 2002).[3] Among other disagreements, normals and queers radically disagree on the importance of access to the institution of marriage (Warner 1999, 81–147).[4] Normals want to be just like straight people—married, often monogamously, and interested in building a traditional family with one intimate partner. For these normals, access to marriage would make for "good gays—the kind who would not challenge the norms of straight culture, who would not flaunt their sexuality, and who would not insist on living differently from ordinary folk" (Warner 1999, 113).

The opinion in *Obergefell* appears to have been written for, and on behalf of, these normals insofar as the legal reasoning offered in the opinion repeatedly invokes the importance of dyadic romantic love, fidelity, children, parenting, and traditional families. In other words, the opinion endorses a particular, assimilationist, conception of the good intimate life—one that is rife with, as I illustrate below, amatonormativity and repronormativity. In doing so, it ends up misrecognizing the queer-identified and the non-assimilationist. Consequently, it comes across as partisan, arbitrary, and deeply invested in the opinion's consequences for law and public policy.

3.2.1 Amatonormativity

The neologism "amatonormativity" is Elizabeth Brake's; she uses the term to signify "the assumptions that a central, exclusive, amorous relationship is normal for humans, in that it is a universally shared goal, and that such a relationship is normative, in that it *should* be aimed at in preference to other relationship types" (Brake 2012, 89, emphasis in the original).[5] This not only results directly in a form of discrimination that might be called "singlism" (Brake 2012, 97; DePaulo 2007; Morris et al. 2008), a phenomenon in which "single people in contemporary American society continue to be stigmatized" (Morris et al. 2008, 166), but also produces prejudice against those who are ethically or consensually non-monogamous (Brake 2012, 91).[6] This "cult of the couple" (DePaulo and Morris 2005, 58) also devalorizes caregiving relationships that are non-romantic and/or non-familial in nature. The amatonormative position attaches respectability to those who find themselves, or claim to be, in romantic relationships with one other person and effectively renders inferior the experiences of those people who are not in and/or are not looking to be in a dyadic romantic relationship. In this sense, having a single and committed romantic partner in America is like having a job. If you don't have one, you are nonetheless aware of the social expectation that you should at least be looking for one. Such injunctions are, of course, ubiquitous and indeed constitute an instance of what Iris Marion Young calls "cultural imperialism"—the universalization of a dominant group's experience and social practices that renders other perspectives invisible and/or inferior (Young 1990, 58–61).

Throughout the majority opinion in *Obergefell*, Justice Kennedy makes what appears to be a strategic use of amatonormative language to deliver an emotionally charged appeal for marriage equality that is presumably intended to cut across ideological and other divides. For Justice Kennedy, any amorous couple—straight or gay—that finds itself in a romantic dyad should be celebrated because of its members' shared interest in the "highest" ideals of love, fidelity, devotion, sacrifice, and family:

> No union is more profound than marriage, for it embodies the highest ideals of love, fidelity, devotion, sacrifice, and family.... As some of the petitioners in these cases demonstrate, marriage embodies a love that may endure even past death. It would misunderstand these men and women to say they disrespect the idea of marriage. Their plea is that they

> do respect it, respect it so deeply that they seek to find its fulfillment for themselves. Their hope is not to be condemned to live in loneliness, excluded from one of civilization's oldest institutions. They ask for *equal dignity* in the eyes of the law. The Constitution grants them that right. (Kennedy 2015, 28)

As Sara Ahmed notes, in the context of Islamophobic and racist utterances and the War on Terror, words can have "problematic proximities," (Ahmed 2011, 199 and *passim*) whose "stickiness…congeals into an attribute" (Ahmed 2011, 125) through "repetition of associations" (Ahmed 2011, 119 and *passim*). The conflation here of the "highest ideals of love, fidelity, devotion, sacrifice, and family" with "marriage" produces a linguistic slippage that makes it sound like unmarried couples[7] are unable to "embody" these ideals. But, of course, as an empirical matter, this proposition is misleading no matter how one defines abstract conceptions like "devotion" and "sacrifice."

While it is not the case that Justice Kennedy's explicit intention is to insinuate that unmarried couples lack such ideals, the institution of marriage is nonetheless positioned here as one with idealistic and indeed "sacramental connotations" (Brake 2012, 14) that unmarried couples simply cannot aspire to. In addition, no justification is provided here for why a list of the "highest ideals" contains items like love,[8] fidelity, devotion, sacrifice, and family but excludes other items like justice, fairness, equality, duty, patriotism, and freedom. Equally, if love can indeed sometimes "endure even past death," surely it is in no further need of being anointed and sanctified by the marriage contract. The reasoning presented here has it backward: It is the marriage contract that would need to attach itself to this highest kind of love in order to enhance *its* dignity, not the other way around. One of these things is eternal and profound, the other an artifact of a specific bureaucracy.

It is also no small irony that in an opinion adorned with the loftiest of language about individual dignity, autonomy, and the related harms and injuries of being "demeaned,"[9] Justice Kennedy himself implies that without marriage one might be "condemned to live in loneliness" (Kennedy 2015, 28). In doing so, he provides an unabashed endorsement of what he considers the good intimate life: The amatonormative life, and one that shores up the conception of the life lived in a dyadic romantic relationship as somehow more privileged (and socially respectable) than any other conception of a good life filled with intimacy.

But, as anyone who is married knows well, it may or may not be the case that marriage removes loneliness, and not all marriages are based on love.

Some marriages are indeed arranged and/or otherwise transactional, and even the federal judiciary recognizes at least some transactional marriages.[10] The history of marriage is in fact rife with transactional alliances—such as the merging of real estate and/or dominions held by two families, building collective security arrangements between kingdoms, property transactions (including artifacts in the form of dowries and trousseaus), coverture, the incurring of reciprocal obligations for caregiving and non-abandonment, the guarantee of inheritance and title for offspring, and so on and so forth (Pateman 1988, especially 154–188; Cott 1998, 1440–1474; Warner 1999, especially 117–126; Josephson 2005, especially 275–277; Brake 2012; Ghosh 2017, 2018). The evolution of the modern "pre-nup" is only the latest iteration of a formal recognition of the widely (although often tacitly) acknowledged fact that intimacies, whether sexual or romantic, are not immune to, or indemnified from, transactionalism.

Furthermore, intimate relationships include all sorts of familial formations (Ettelbrick and Shapiro 2004, 476; Ghosh 2018).[11] Ordinary individuals routinely choose to conduct their intimate lives in an endless variety of ways, and the ideal of a deeply committed romantic couple, locked in an everlasting dyad, hardly represents a self-evident, or even self-justifying, norm. The affluent are more likely to get married than the poor (Rampell 2012; Perry 2014; Cook 2015). In 2015, the marriage rate in the United States was the lowest it had ever been in history (Cook 2015). Divorce is common. Even among those who are married, some couples are asexual partners, others maintain separate domiciles or keep their property disentangled. Yet others choose to remain single, some are "quirkyalones" (Brake 2012, 89), some are polyamorous, some live in urban tribes, some in child-rearing support networks, adult care networks, or informal associations of friends or relatives, and some might even believe in polyfidelity, or "ethical nonmonogamy" (Brake 2012, 91; X 2015; Hawkins et al. 2017). In a plural society, the thriving list of such intimacies is practically inexhaustible.

Sexual exclusivity is also, and has always been, an unenforceable norm, and "consensual non-exclusivity" (Macedo 2015, 17) can be found everywhere. Yet, *Obergefell* reminds us that one of the plaintiffs, James Obergefell, and his late partner John Arthur "fell in love and started a life together, establishing a lasting, committed relation" (Kennedy 2015, 4).

It also announces that the plaintiffs are not intent upon demeaning the "revered idea and reality of marriage" (Kennedy 2015, 4). Instead, for the petitioners, marriage is of "enduring importance" (Kennedy 2015, 4). They have "respect" and "need" for marriage's "privileges and responsibilities" and the "immutable nature" of this respect, and this need "dictates that same-sex marriage is their only real path to this profound commitment" (Kennedy 2015, 4). In other words, these petitioners are trying to assimilate into a culture that privileges marriage and, for the Court, it is laudable that these gays and lesbians are assimilationist. They realize they have been unjustly excluded from this institution for centuries, but they are asking nicely and making a good case for their admission into this "revered idea and reality of marriage" (Kennedy 2015, 4) and, *a fortiori*, we should grant them their wish.

However, many see marriage as a flawed institution, and one that can be "claustrophobic," "overburdening," and replete with "impossible expectations" (W. Brown 2004, 89–90). Moreover, as Justice Scalia unforgettably puts it, marriage can "abridge," rather than expand, freedom of intimacy (Scalia 2015, 8).[12] It is also well established in social science research as well as in philosophy that marriage has been, for most of history and in most cultural settings, historically undergirded by racist assumptions (in the United States) (Josephson 2005, especially 275–276; Brake 2012, 11), and a medium of accumulation of the products of women's domestic labor (Pateman 1988, 133; Josephson 2005, 276). This is why many of marriage's critics appreciate why "marriage has long been the focus of radical-feminist revulsion" (Ettelbrick 1992 [1989], 20). As a mark of resistance, these critics, both radical feminists and others, have long affirmed the practice of forming relationships and families that do not fit the traditional marriage mold. They see this as liberating and many even call for the eradication of state recognition of marriage (see, e.g., Kinsley 2003; Metz 2004, 2010; Ackelsberg and Plaskow 2004; March 2010; Chambers 2013; Ghosh 2017, 2018). As Katherine Franke points out: "What's difficult to explain is that for some lesbians and gay men, having our relationships sanctioned and regulated by the state is hardly something to celebrate. It was [after all] only a few years ago that we were criminals in the eyes of the law simply because of whom we loved" (Franke 2011).

Given these controversies about marriage, it is hard to see why the Court would endorse the "revered idea and reality of marriage" (Kennedy 2015, 4) to resolve a polarizing dispute about an equal rights claim emanating from a historically marginalized group. I will return to this discussion in the concluding section of this essay. But before that, in the next section, I discuss the trope of repronormativity in *Obergefell*. Apart from the insistence, as described in detail in this section, that there is only one kind of love—dyadic romantic love—that is worthy of respect when it comes to the formation of intimate partnerships, the Court in *Obergefell* also insists on the vital role of children and parenting to ground a justification for marriage equality. In doing so, it aggressively endorses a conception of the good, traditional, and nuclear, family. As a result, it misrecognizes the experiences of all those who are not, or have not been, members of traditional families.

3.2.2 *Repronormativity*

One of the foundational premises of Justice Kennedy's argument in *Obergefell* is the discussion of harm and humiliation caused to the children of same-sex couples that wish to marry and are denied marriage rights by the state (Kennedy 2015, 15). This section of the opinion, however, inaugurates a series of linguistic slippages that, in effect, amount to a repronormative set of injunctions at the heart of the decision (on repronormativity, see Franke [2009, 30–38], Zivi [2014, 291] and *passim*).[13] Consequently, the opinion ends up reifying what Karen Zivi accurately suggested a year before *Obergefell* was decided: "a historical American understanding of *good citizenship* that links the right to marry with the proper reproduction of children and social norms and this, in turn, with the health and identity of the nation" (Zivi 2014, 291).

Closely related to heteronormativity and amatonormativity, repronormativity is a critical term that signifies a form of cultural imperialism and, just as in the case of the other two terms, it is employed by many theorists to identify a social phenomenon in which the dominant culture's attachment to the role of biology, reproduction, and child-rearing in family formations is normalized and imposed on all others (Franke 2009, 30–38; Zivi 2014, 291). A relatively nascent addition to the canon of critical theory, the idea fuses insights from the feminist theory of motherhood with insights drawn from the queer and feminist critique of heteronormativity. It interrogates the occlusion of a positive theory of female sexuality as well as the social forces that foreground (in part by incentivizing) "the reproductive uses of women's sexual bodies" (Franke 2009, 31). In this context, Franke (2009) has also provocatively suggested:

"Being a de-eroticized mother cannot be the only viable alternative to being a slut or celibate" (2009, 42). Particularly in the context of marriage equality litigation in the United States, repronormativity refers to:

> The network of ideas and practices, policies, and economic conditions that promote biological and cultural reproduction as the primary goal for adults, making parenthood a necessary and celebrated practice vital to individual self-fulfillment and national stability. Whereas reprosexuality draws our attention to the heteronormativity at the heart of this network and to the obfuscation of the procreative and parenting practices of gay couples, repronormativity expands the focus to shed light on the ways in which these discourses have shifted so as to *include* gays and lesbians. (Zivi 2014, 293–294)

Amatonormativity and repronormativity are, in other words, heteronormativity with a "gay spin" (Bedi, quoted in Macedo [2015, 10]). They posit that in a progressive and newly pro-marriage equality United States, gays and lesbians are allowed to subvert whatever traditional gender roles they want to, but they would be foolhardy indeed to destabilize the traditional notion of the ideal family—always already presented as a nuclear family, headed by a dyadic, amorous, romantic couple, steeped in fidelity as well as parental obligations (even as parenthood is elaborately re-characterized as not compulsorily biological).

Widespread social acceptance of this kind of repronormativity produces many harms. As in the case of other forms of cultural imperialism, it makes inferior, invisible, or somehow less noteworthy and socially respectable the experiences of childless couples as well as single people (especially women) who are not parents. It does so principally by marking them as culpable of multiple social sins, such as not having done their part to form an ideal family, and not having the ability to empathize with the experiences of people who do in fact have parental responsibilities. It is especially demeaning for childless women of reproductive age (or those who are older) because these women have to live with the specter of a collective social presumption of—as well as pity for and disapproval of—their infertility and/or general undesirability.[14]

This cultural norm enables people who are parents to demand, and routinely obtain, all sorts of accommodations in their discharge of professional duties in the name of work–family balance and to the occlusion of work–life balance (Keeney et al. 2013; also see Henion and Ryan 2013;

Schachter 2013). Thus, workers and professionals who are parents are allowed to leave official meetings early (or arrive late) on the understanding that they experience suffering when they cannot attend to the needs of their children as a result of conflict with work-related obligations. It is true that children need their parents by their side (when they are sick, e.g., or, say, when they are participating in a school play) and that not being able to meet their children's needs inevitably causes most parents considerable suffering. But it is also the case that individuals experience suffering when they cannot attend to, say, personal education, or their health, or even, in some cases, leisure activities. There is no *reasonable* way to adjudicate if one of these forms of suffering is greater than the other, unless one takes it as axiomatic that parents attending to children's needs somehow deserve a set of accommodations that others are simply not entitled to. And yet, we live in a social context in which this proposition is, in fact, taken as axiomatic. As a result, non-parents' concerns are routinely taken less seriously than the individuals who claim they have parental obligations. Thus, "people without children find their own non-work activities treated as less important than the family activities of colleagues with children" (Schachter 2013). This privileging of parenting responsibilities also absolves those who raise children of various obligations, as in cases when, for example, their childless siblings bear a disproportionate burden and responsibility of caregiving for their own parents.[15]

Given these various asymmetries, inequities, and even oppressive tendencies of repronormativity, it is disheartening to see its presence at the very center of the *Obergefell* decision. The actual text of the opinion, thus, ends up marginalizing and devaluing, the experiences of all those children who have grown up in non-traditional households, with divorced, unmarried, serially married, and/or single parents. Here is a case in point:

> Without the recognition, stability, and predictability marriage offers, [the unmarried same-sex couples'] children suffer the stigma of knowing their families are somehow lesser. They also suffer the significant material costs of being raised by unmarried parents, relegated through no fault of their own to a more difficult and uncertain family life. The marriage laws at issue here thus harm and humiliate the children of same-sex couples. ... That is not to say the right to marry is less meaningful for those who do not or cannot have children. (Kennedy 2015, 15)

One can imagine that the use of the phrase "material costs" refers to tax breaks that married couples get, which, in turn, make them financially better off than similarly situated unmarried couples or single parents. But, what precisely constitutes, one might ask, being "relegated" to this "more difficult and uncertain family life" as a result of these material costs? And even if this claim were true, would children growing up in single-parent households or households with unmarried parents *invariably* suffer "more difficult and uncertain" family lives than those who grow up with married and cohabiting parents? What about those whose parents have had several marriages? Or those who grow up with step-parents? Satisfactory answers to these questions can never be supplied because we are never told what these difficulties and uncertainties, specifically, are. But the "judgment" of the opinion is clear: Married parents are good for children. In other words, there is one "good" way to form a family.

The denial of marriage rights, *Obergefell* tells us, leads to children of gays and lesbians suffering from the "stigma of knowing their families are somehow lesser," because they lack the "recognition, stability, and predictability marriage offers" (Kennedy 2015, 15). It follows, then, that at least a version of this kind of suffering is experienced by the children of all those people who are unmarried and/or single. But if the objective of the state is to remove this stigma, marriage equality is hardly the first procedural step in this direction; it in fact requires a wholesale changing of the hearts and minds of people. Indeed, it requires the eradication of the repronormative cultural assumptions about what constitutes an ideal family, together with the social privileging of these family formations, which is what the opinion itself appears to be invested in preserving.

In *Obergefell*, the Court need only have upheld or struck down the state bans on same-sex marriage. In order to do so, it was not required of it to deploy this language of repronormativity. Yet the opinion perseveres with a wholehearted endorsement of repronormativity as it characterizes the protection of children from harm and humiliation as a "central premise" of the right to marry. It bears quoting this section at length here:

> [One] basis for protecting the right to marry is that it safeguards children and families and thus draws meaning from related rights of childrearing, procreation, and education.... By giving recognition and legal structure to their parents' relationship, marriage allows children "to understand

> the integrity and closeness of their own family and its concord with other families in their community and in their daily lives." *Windsor*, *supra*, at ___ (slip op., at 23). Marriage also affords the permanency and stability important to children's *best interests*.... Gays and lesbians can create loving, supportive families. Excluding same-sex couples from marriage thus conflicts with a *central premise* of the right to marry. (Kennedy 2015, 14–15, emphasis mine)

The unsustainability of the claims made here becomes apparent the instant one attempts to evaluate or falsify them. Two controversial suggestions, in particular, stand out. The first is the misguided proposition that if your parents are not married, it would be difficult for you to "understand the integrity and closeness of [your] family," even though unmarried gays and lesbians do, in fact, have the ability to create "loving, supportive families." One can, of course, assert all sorts of things about abstractions like integrity and closeness of family ties as articles of faith, or arrive at these conclusions on the basis of one's personal history or experiences, or even profess them as a "conception of the good," but these propositions do not admit of any hypothesis-testing, operationalization of variables, evidence-based reasoning, argumentation, or even, surprisingly, logic.

These statements also render as inferior, and less socially respectable, the life choices of those parents who voluntarily elected to never marry, those parents who live apart or who ended their marriages in divorce, and indeed the lives of those children who (invariably involuntarily) grew up in households where their parents were not married and/or living together.

The Court implies that if your parents are divorced or elected to never get married, then they have effectively deprived you of "permanency and stability." But permanency and stability in what domains? The citation that follows the phrase is to pages 22–27 of an amicus brief (Smith et al. 2015) which, in turn, explicitly states the following: "The *permanency*, consistency, and *stability* inherent in the parent-child relationship has been recognized by the states as securing children's *best interests* in the *adoption*, *custody*, and *visitation* contexts" (Smith et al. 2015, 22, emphasis mine).[16] However, unlike the amicus brief, nothing in *Obergefell* tells us what, precisely, Justice Kennedy has in mind when he is referring to children's "best interests." Is he talking about children's best interests in these specific contexts—of adoption, custody, or visitation? Or is he talking about children's "best interests" *per se*? Few would dispute the former. But the latter would be a more controversial suggestion.

To be sure, some social scientific studies do suggest that children living in "two-*biological*-parent cohabiting" families, in certain situations, experience worse "outcomes" when measured for "well-being" than those living with "two *biological* married parents" (Brown 2004, 351, emphasis mine). These findings, however, say nothing about gay couples. In addition, couples choose to marry—or not, or to separate, or to sometimes get back together—for a range of competing and often interrelated reasons, and children's interests (best or otherwise) constitute only one of them. Therefore, to position the "best interests" of children at the heart of the opinion is to elide the complex set of reasons that animate couples' desire to not be married and/or to not cohabit, and to didactically codify the Court's disapproval of those who do not look after the unspecified "best interests" of children. Thus, by stipulating a nexus between reproduction/child-rearing and wedlock the Court upholds the dominant culture's understanding of family formation and sets it up as a norm to which all ought to aspire.

So far, I have engaged with a critique of the *Obergefell* opinion because it tries to normify conduct by endorsing a conception of the good life. But what would a judgment that did not endorse such a conception look like? In the next section, I demonstrate that a turn to decisional minimalism would have enabled the Court to avoid the rhetorical pitfalls I have identified and critiqued above.

3.3 Decisional Minimalism as Non-endorsement

The opinion in *Obergefell* should have been written as a quintessential example of non-endorsement. One form such a language of non-endorsement could have taken would very much look like what Cass Sunstein has called decisional minimalism—a judicial strategy that attempts to solve one case at a time, leave several things undecided, and issue a narrow opinion that makes "it possible to obtain agreement where agreement is necessary, [and makes] it unnecessary to obtain agreement where agreement is impossible" (Sunstein 1994, 1743, emphasis removed). Such strategies reduce the burden on judicial decisions and make judicial errors less frequent and less damaging (Sunstein 1999, 4). This approach also leaves ample room for democratic deliberation by avoiding acts of deciding constitutional questions (Sunstein 1999, 4) and by the deployment of a "constructive use of silence" (Sunstein 1999, 5). These strategies are often predicated on agreements that are incompletely theorized and that leave "victorious litigants with less than they might have won and divests defeated litigants of less than they might have lost" (Bybee and Ghosh 2009, 133). In so doing, they preserve stability and temper conflict in deeply polarizing radical disputes (Sunstein 1994, 1735, 8n).

The marriage equality debate in the United States represents just the sort of polarizing moral conflict that Sunstein had in mind when he proposed the idea of incompletely theorized agreement. These are conflicts in which parties that most strongly affirm their position on either side of this dispute are "fundamentally"[17] opposed to the other's views as a result of their deepest convictions.[18] As Sunstein characterizes them, these are "apparently intractable social disagreements on a wide range of first principles" (Sunstein 1994, 1735).

Such disputes are ubiquitous in pluralistic societies because such polities necessarily comprise members with "deep differences" (Bybee and Ghosh 2009, 138; Ghosh 2013, 55) who have radically incommensurable views on politics, economics, religious beliefs, and social and cultural values. We confront examples of such radical disputes everywhere: abortion, same-sex marriage, free markets, animal sacrifice, veiling, female genital mutilation, polygamy, arranged marriages, child marriage, undocumented/illegal immigrants, intelligent design/creationism, affirmative action, bilingualism, school prayer, honor killings, and so on. Because the disputing parties cannot agree on basic principles and assumptions, we end up with scenarios where what is deemed to be perfectly acceptable—in some cases, even required of individuals—in one cultural or subcultural context is seen as entirely unacceptable by those who find themselves outside of that context. The rejection of any universal declaration of "human rights" in the name of cultural relativism is a version of this problem, and one that leads Shashi Tharoor (Tharoor 1999) to, only part-facetiously, ask: "when you stop a man in traditional dress from beating his wife, are you upholding her human rights or violating his?"

Under conditions of deep difference, it is extraordinarily difficult to stipulate any general adjudicatory principles the application of which would resolve these conflicts, and each proposed mechanism of settlement appears to leave critical room for improvement. Nonetheless, various mechanisms for the resolution, or at least tempering, of radical disputes have indeed been proposed. From within political liberalism, for example, the response, frequently, is that an impartial settlement on the basis of public reason will resolve these conflicts. In this view, public reason is supposed to be a form of political reasoning predicated not on any comprehensive doctrine but instead on a universal grammar marked by evidence-based reasoning and argumentation that are, presumptively, intelligible to all parties (Rawls 1996; also see Larmore 2002; Frohock 2006a; Freeman 2004; Gutmann and Thompson 1998). Thus, citizens who have deep moral disagreements are asked to "continue to reason together to reach mutually acceptable decisions" and, in doing so, partake in a flourishing "deliberative democracy" (Gutmann and Thompson 1998, 1).

As Stanley Fish has demonstrated, however, this sort of thing rarely happens when the parties to the dispute are involved in a disagreement that is "fundamental" (Fish 1997a, 388) to their worldview and where disagreements are "marked by the refusal of either party to listen to reason" (Fish 1997a, 388). For Fish, "persons embedded within *different* discursive systems will not be able to hear the other's reasons *as* reasons, but only as errors or even delusions" (Fish 1994, 136). It is not surprising therefore that public reason has been accused of "invoking" reason without "giving" any, and thus exhibiting a self-justification of "breathtaking circularity" (Campos 1994, 1821). Equally, it has been discovered to be a "comprehensive doctrine" in itself even as it rejects principles derived from comprehensive doctrines (Owen 2001, 121–127; Fish 1994, 134–138; George 1997, 2479–2480). Reason, it turns out, is also desperately ill-equipped to adjudicate disputes, especially in cases that most require governance, such as, for example, disputes involving church and state (see, e.g., Frohock [2006b]; Fish [1997b]). Finally, reasonableness is said to serve the same performative function in Rawls's theory that the term "God" does in dogmatic religious argument (Campos 1994, 1818).[19]

Some have proposed, *contra* Rawls, that disputing parties with radical differences will try to achieve nothing but a *modus vivendi* (Frohock 2006a, 30), and, with this in mind, they suggest a range of different, often pragmatic, approaches to conflict resolution (see, e.g., Posner's [2003] concept of "everyday pragmatism"). One such approach suggests wholeheartedly embracing the fact that *realpolitik* (strategic interactions between nation-states) teaches us important lessons about the balance of power and conflict resolution across deep divides (Frohock 2006a). Another approach suggests the use of a little "hypocrisy" as well as "courtesy" in our social interactions with an eye toward enabling "social lubrication" so that people can get along (Bybee 2005). Yet another approach abandons the project of coming up with general principles of adjudication and instead draws from real-world experiences of what disputing parties inevitably *do*. Thus, Stanley Fish, invoking Charles Taylor, suggests that parties in these conflicts should continue doing what they would be doing anyway—that is, improvise, on the basis of "inspired adhoccery" (Fish 1997a). This kind of improvisation appears to consist of the following plan: Do whatever you can to defeat your enemy, including, biding your time when you think you might lose, and waiting to strike your enemy until you think you can defeat them. In this view, adherence to your convictions—and winning—is all that matters; there are no general principles to be had.

To be sure, the Supreme Court of the United States cannot declare as a principle, the adoption of a strategy such as one based on inspired adhoccery when it adjudicates polarizing disputes involving questions like marriage equality. However, the Court also need not, and routinely does not, act like what Rawls has called the "exemplar of public reason" (Rawls 1996, 231–240; also see Freeman 2004; Bybee and Ghosh 2009). Legal realists have long noted that judges routinely act "politically" and objective judicial reasoning does not always issue from the high bench (Bybee 2010, 3–4; also see Holmes 1897, 465–466). Judicial hypocrisy, it turns out, is ubiquitous and not always a bad thing (Bybee 2010).

In this context, Cass Sunstein's prescriptive as well as descriptive approach rooted in decisional minimalism makes a great deal of sense. As indicated above, Sunstein has famously suggested that the Supreme Court, in the face of deeply dividing conflicts that seem apparently intractable, often relies on a minimalist strategy characterized by great judicial restraint and the issuance of incremental opinions (Sunstein 1999). These minimalist opinions have two key attributes: They are both narrow and shallow. They are narrow in the sense that they only relate to the specific case at hand, and avoid the establishment of sweeping new laws that affect all similarly situated cases; and shallow, in the sense that they offer "incompletely theorized agreement" (Sunstein 1994, 1999; also see Bybee and Ghosh 2009) that do not seek to resolve the totality of all aspects of the specific dispute and instead leaves room for democratic decision-making to attend to those dimensions of the dispute that are not critically important for the Court to attend to.

The application of such an approach in *Obergefell* would have entailed relying exclusively on existing jurisprudence on the rights of sexual minorities and marriage and refraining from any articulations whose discursive reach was broader than the specific issue at hand (Yoshino 2015, 147). Thus, the majority in *Obergefell* could have ruled that state bans on same-sex marriage are violative of the Equal Protection Clause of the Fourteenth Amendment in a way that is similar to Virginia's former ban on interracial marriage, which the Court struck down in *Loving v. Virginia* (1967) as an instance of "invidious racial discrimination" (Warren 1967, 8 and *passim*). Race being a suspect classification meant that, in *Loving*, the Court could incontrovertibly impose the highest level of judicial scrutiny to adjudicate the issue.

In the case of discrimination against gays and lesbians, this would introduce an additional layer of complexity because discriminatory statutes targeting gays and lesbians have not been, so far, accorded a heightened level of judicial scrutiny by the Court (Stone 2015). Yet, the Court has repeatedly found bans on same-sex intimate conduct and marriage to be unconstitutional even under the "highly deferential" rational basis standard (Stone 2015).[20] Additionally, the Court could have, if it so chose, also decided whether bans on same-sex marriage constitute "animus."[21] Alternatively, the opinion could have relied exclusively, and simply, on the argument that marriage is a fundamental right protected by the Due Process clause of the Fourteenth Amendment and that it was impermissible under the Constitution for a state to deny any intimate couple their fundamental right to marry (Gerstmann 2008).

Instead, *Obergefell* announces the emergence of a "sweeping" (Yoshino 2015, 147) new doctrine as the culmination of a long line of opinions related to sexuality, privacy, and dignity that Justice Kennedy has authored since *Planned Parenthood v. Casey* (1992) (Rosen 2006).[22] This doctrine finds the Equal Protection and Due Process clauses of the Fourteenth Amendment to be "wound" (Tribe 2015, 17; also see Yoshino 2015, 148) in a way that indicates the presence of a right to equal dignity, that, incidentally, is nowhere enshrined in the Constitution. Over the last three decades or so, Justice Kennedy has recognized dignity interests in various other cases, including *Lawrence v. Texas* (2003), a decision that made sodomy laws unconstitutional in the United States. It is this discovery, by interpretation, of a new constitutional right to support a judicial outcome in a deeply controversial dispute that makes this decision so very "maximalist"—indeed, it is a "game changer for substantive due process jurisprudence" (Yoshino 2015, 148). While it is true that the right to dignity itself is mentioned in the

Universal Declaration of Human Rights and it is taken very seriously in international human rights discourse, it is also true that it is very difficult to enumerate the phrase's constitutive elements (United Nations 1948).

In addition, the establishment of a right to equal dignity opens up the problematic possibility that it is going to run up against other constitutional guarantees. Consider the case of free speech jurisprudence in the United States. Over the course of the twentieth century, the Supreme Court has steadily chipped away speech proscriptions and adopted a highly libertarian approach to free speech jurisprudence. Thus, barring certain very selected categories of speech like those likely to produce "imminent lawless action," most things can generally be freely said; this includes symbolic speech ranging from burning a cross and tossing it into the backyard of an African-American family (*R.A.V. v. City of St. Paul* [1992]) to burning the American flag as a gesture of political protest (*Texas v. Johnson* [1989]). For the press, prohibitions on "prior restraint" (*Near v. Minnesota* [1931]) and the burden of proof on the part of the plaintiff to prove "actual malice" (*New York Times Co. v. Sullivan* [1964]) on the part of the publication in cases of defamation, together make it generally possible for publications to be securely protected against First Amendment encroachments (see also, *Hustler Magazine Inc. v. Falwell* [1988]). Finally, as a practical matter, hate speech is protected under the Constitution even though hate crimes are not (see, e.g., *Brandenburg v. Ohio* [1969] and *Snyder v. Phelps* [2011]).

What happens to free speech jurisprudence, though, when the Court decides that dignity is a constitutional right guaranteed by the Fourteenth Amendment? If the doctrine of equal dignity becomes a matter of settled law, it is hard to see how one person's right to dignity will not collide with another person's right to free speech. The Court will inevitably have to take one side or another in a myriad such dignity-versus-freedom of speech disputes, and might very well, in the process of doing so, end up generating an ever-growing list of radical disputes.

All this is not to say that there is no such thing as a right to equal dignity. It is also not to say that "originalism" or "textualism" (Scalia 1997; Barnett 2017), is the only permissible reading of the law, or that interpretations of the Constitution in light of changing circumstances—that is, an adherence to the theory of a "living constitution"—should never be permissible (Barnett 2017). But it is dangerously ill-advised to propose the discovery of a novel constitutional right at the same time as the Court issues an opinion that does not furnish a fully worked out theory grounding its legal reasoning and, in so doing, sides with one of the partisans in a deeply moral conflict. This takes away even a veneer of impartiality. What was needed in *Obergefell* was decisional minimalism, as a signifier of the Court's relative neutrality, and not a sweeping new doctrine. Instead, the Court in *Obergefell* has transparently sided with one of the disputants (in this case, marriage equality proponents, while ignoring critiques of that position from within the queer community itself) in a deeply polarizing moral conflict. As a result, the opinion has reconfirmed every suspicion of unfairness that LGBT+ rights opponents have against the Court. Consequently, in all likelihood, it has escalated hostility toward this already marginalized group.

As Jeffrey Rosen has suggested, the last time the Court invoked a novel constitutional right to settle a deeply moral conflict was in *Roe v. Wade* (1973) when the Court "unilaterally leaped ahead of a national consensus" (Rosen 2006, 81–113, especially 90–103; the quote appears on 90). In this case, the right to "privacy," discovered by the Court in the penumbras and emanations of the Constitution in *Griswold v. Connecticut* (1965), was invoked as the Court struck down state statutes that prohibited first semester abortions. A small majority of the population at the time agreed with *Roe*'s central holding, but supermajorities wanted some provisions like spousal notification laws, parental notifications laws, informed consent requirements, and so on—which were all struck down by lower courts, citing *Roe*, in the ensuing years. This generated, as Rosen carefully documents, a backlash against abortion rights, and eventually produced, by 1992, a judicial retreat on *Roe* (Rosen 2006, 90–103). The problem was not that *Roe* was incorrectly decided but instead that it was not minimalist—in fact, it did not even try to be so. It appeared to explicitly side with one partisan outcome in a deeply moral conflict. In other words, it did not *appear* neutral. As a result, as Justice Ruth Bader Ginsburg describes it: "The sweep and detail of the opinion stimulated the mobilization of a right-to-life movement and an attendant reaction in Congress and state legislatures" (Ginsberg 1985, 375).

Cass Sunstein, in his analysis of a line of "privacy" cases from *Griswold v. Connecticut* to *Lawrence v. Texas*, has suggested that he would rather do away with "privacy" altogether (Fleming and McClain 2013, 211). Instead, he argues, the Court should have used some other legal principle, such as desuetude or the Equal Protection Clause to engender agreement on the results of some of these decisions. One example of this would be *Roe*, in which Sunstein thinks equal protection principles would have been less "adventurous" and provide a more "secure basis" for the decision (Sunstein 1993, 312). Broad rulings in these cases, he suggests, erode the possibility of democratic decision-making and create the possibility of backlash and escalates conflict.

On the other hand, James Fleming and Linda McClain have proposed that Sunstein exaggerates this fear of backlash (Fleming and McClain 2013, 230–232). But as they themselves indicate, a comparison of the Vermont Supreme Court's decision in *Baker v. State of Vermont* (1999) and the Massachusetts Supreme Judicial Court's decision in *Goodridge v. Department of Public Health* (2003) may be instructive in analyzing this claim. When the Vermont Supreme Court, in *Baker v. State of Vermont* (1999), found the denial of marriage rights for same-sex couples to be in violation of the State Constitution's Common Benefits Clause, it left it to the Vermont legislature to remedy the violation (Fleming and McClain 2013, 220). It is possible that this deference to democratic deliberation might have enabled Vermont to avoid the backlash generated by the Hawaii Supreme Court's decision in *Baehr v. Miike* (originally *Baker v. Lewin*) (Fleming and McClain 2013, 220). As this latter case moved through the state court system throughout the 1990s, Hawaii passed a state constitutional amendment that led to the eventual dismissal of the case. It also triggered a spate of other state constitutional amendments banning same-sex marriage as well as the federal Defense of Marriage Act (1996). The House Judiciary Committee, in fact, issued a report calling for DOMA as a response to *Baehr* (US House of Representatives 1996).

Similarly, in 2003, when the Massachusetts Supreme Judicial Court issued its decision in *Goodridge*, instating state marriage equality for the first time, it "redefined the common law to construe marriage as a 'voluntary union of two persons as spouses, to the exclusion of all others'" (Ireland 2010, 1420). In the aftermath of the decision—as Senior Associate Justice of the Massachusetts Supreme Judicial Court, and one of the justices who joined the majority in *Goodridge*, the Hon. Roderick L. Ireland describes it—there was significant backlash: The Massachusetts Senate asked the Court for an advisory opinion on whether or not providing civil unions would satisfy the state's constitutional requirements (this proposal was rejected by the Court); there were various lawsuits and petitions opposing the decision; an initiative petition was sponsored to amend the Constitution in 2006 (it eventually failed in the Massachusetts legislature on a required second vote); the Court was subjected to various kinds of name-calling; and some members of the Court even received death threats (Ireland 2010, 1421).

President George W. Bush criticized the decision and invoked the "sanctity of marriage" in his State of the Union message of 2004 (Bush 2004). The Bush administration also supported a federal constitutional amendment restricting marriage to opposite-sex couples (Allen and Cooperman 2004). Even Fleming and McClain admit that "not a word was heard" (Fleming and McClain 2013, 222–223) of the 1999 *Baker* decision and Vermont's subsequent institution of civil unions in 2000 during the 2000 presidential election, while the outcome of the 2004 presidential election could be explained at least in part by the backlash to the Massachusetts Supreme Court's *Goodridge* decision in 2003.[23]

We can safely say, with Marx, that "all great, world-historical facts and personages occur, as it were, twice" (Marx 1978 [1852], 594). Just as it did in the case of *Roe*, *Obergefell* is likely to generate a similar and widespread backlash against LGBT+ rights across the 50 states, in spheres ranging from religious exemptions for the provision of services, employment non-discrimination, and many others. In 2016, the North Carolina state legislature passed a bill prohibiting transgender people from using bathrooms and locker rooms that do not match their sex/gender on their birth certificates. The same year, *The New York Times* reported on "heartbreaking" levels of violence against gay and lesbian high school students (Hoffman 2016). In 2017, a contentious debate started in Texas about a similar bill that would restrict some forms of bathroom access for transgender people (National Public Radio 2017). Meanwhile, President Trump, during his first year in office has revoked a set of guidelines issued by the Obama White House that allowed transgender students the right to use the bathroom of their choice (Trotta 2017). Finally, in 2018, according to a GLAAD "Accelerating Acceptance" survey, for the first time in four years support for LGBT+ people has dropped in all the seven areas the survey measured. According to Jennifer Boylan in *The New York Times*, "the statistics measuring uncomfortability with L.G.B.T.Q. people are right back where they were in 2014" (Boylan 2018).

In its October term 2016, the Supreme Court was scheduled to hear oral arguments in *Gloucester County School Board v. G.G.*—a case involving a transgender student's right to access the bathroom of his choice. However, given the Trump administration's move, the Court vacated the appeals court decision in this case and sent it back to the lower court for re-consideration. In its October term 2017, in *Masterpiece Cakeshop v Colorado Civil Rights Division*, the Court is scheduled to issue an opinion in the case of Jack Phillips, a baker who maintains that it is his "standard business practice not to provide cakes for same-sex weddings" (M. 2017).

It is, as of now, too early to definitively determine whether or not there is an ongoing nationwide backlash to *Obergefell.* But some of the signs (described above) are worrisome. It is also the case that a strategy of decisional minimalism may or may not have prevented *Obergefell* from producing a backlash, such as the one we have seen in the aftermath of *Roe*. However, as I have argued throughout this chapter, it remains the case that the family values rhetoric of *Obergefell* has done quite a bit of disservice to the cause of LGBT+ rights in the United States. It has demeaned and alienated all those of us who cannot or will not fall in line with the opinion's assimilationist injunctions. In addition, its rhetoric has reconfirmed for LGBT+ rights opponents that a liberal and activist Court is taking sides in this deeply polarizing divide. The Court could have, if it so wished, used this opportunity to issue an opinion steeped in decisional minimalism. Doing so would have enabled the Court to eschew the public impression that the Court was partisan. Such a gesture would have gone a long way in tempering the conflict surrounding LGBT+ rights in the United States. Regrettably, however, in *Obergefell*, the Court has self-consciously decided to move in exactly the opposite direction.

Notes

1. As noted in Chapter 2, critical legal theorists have long pointed out that when there is no word for a specific form of oppression in a given cultural setting, it can be disabling in that we cannot identify them and express precisely what is going on. See, for example, the discussion on "Structural Determinism" in Delgado and Stefancic (Delgado and Stefancic 2001, 25–26). A case study of this problem appears in Morris et al. (2008, 165–194). "Amatonormativity" and "repronormativity" are relatively new terms in the critical theory literature and, as I suggest in the remainder of the paper, they are useful terms given the rapidly changing context of sexuality rights discourse in the United States.
2. The discussion in this section appears in Ghosh (2018).
3. On the politics of difference, see Young (1990, 163–173), Fraser (1995), and Ghosh (2013, especially 67–72).

4. Warner also helpfully reminds us that "lived intimacies seldom take the form imposed by marriage" (Warner 1999, 107). Also see, Ettelbrick (1992 [1989], 20–26), Franke (2011) and Ghosh (2017, 2018).
5. Brake also clarifies that the term is broad enough to include the privilege enjoyed by "unmarried cohabitants" and, therefore, more inclusive than the more restrictive term "conjugonormativity" (Brake 2012, 89, 18n).
6. The term "ethical nonmonogamy" represents a variety of ways of living out one's intimate life that includes polyamory, polyfidelity, open marriages, and so on. See, for example, X (2015). Some people also use the term "consensual nonmonogamy" (abbreviated as CNM). See, for example, Hawkins et al. (2017).
7. For the sake of simplicity, I am bracketing out here a discussion of triads and other plural amorous formations.
8. For an interesting discussion of the "political and philosophical construction" of love in western philosophy, see Martel (2001, 2).
9. The word "demean" (or a derivative of it), in fact, appears five times in the majority opinion (Kennedy 2015, 4 [twice], 17, 19 and 22).
10. See, for example, Department of Justice (2012).
11. Even Stephen Macedo, who is an advocate of liberal monogamy and marriage equality, agrees that "a variety of forms of nonmarital caring and caregiving relationships" do, in fact, exist. See Macedo (2015, 9).
12. The quote is from Justice Antonin Scalia's dissent in *Obergefell v. Hodges* (Scalia 2015). He also sardonically adds (in the next line): "Ask the nearest hippie!"
13. On the related concept of "homonormativity," see Puar (2006, 67–88) and Duggan (2002, 175–194); also see, Weber (2016, 108–111) and Ghosh (2016).
14. Obviously, men can lack "fertility" too. But the point here is relevant for women in a way that does not really apply to men.
15. There is some evidence that modern marriage diminishes companionship with relatives, including parents and siblings, other than the spouse—at least in the United States. See Gerstel and Sarkisian (2006, 18).
16. There are a couple of other references to "best interests" in the cited pages, but none that makes a point about "permanency" and "stability."
17. As Stanley Fish has suggested, fundamental differences concern a person's "basic beliefs and commitments" (Fish 1997a, 388).
18. On the nature of such fundamental disagreements, see Fish (1997a), Bybee and Ghosh (2009), and Frohock (2006a, 28–29).
19. In response to these criticisms, many theorists, including Rawls, have proposed reformulations of the idea of public reason. Thus, Rawls offers a "wide" view of public reason in "The Idea of Public Reason Revisited" (Rawls 1997), one that includes the provision that citizens "may call upon their full convictions at any time" (Larmore 2002, 386); also see Patten (2003, 356).

20. As a practical matter, *Obergefell* does not stipulate the level of judicial scrutiny the Court used to find that state bans on same-sex marriage violates the Equal Protection Clause of the Fourteenth Amendment.
21. The Court found the existence of animus in *Romer v. Evans* (1996).
22. Justice Scalia has famously ridiculed this portion of the *Casey* opinion as the "sweet-mystery-of-life" passage. See, *Lawrence v. Texas* (2003).
23. Fleming and McClain do appear, however, to think that the backlash caused by the *Goodridge* decision would have occurred even if it were to be the case that the MA state legislature, and not the courts were to have instated marriage equality in the state (Fleming and McClain 2013, 231).

References

Ackelsberg, Martha, and Judith Plaskow. 2004. "Why We're Not Getting Married." *Keshet Online*. https://www.keshetonline.org/wp-content/uploads/2012/02/Why-Were-Not-Getting-Married.pdf.

Ahmed, Sara. 2011. "Problematic Proximities: Or Why Critiques of Gay Imperialism Matter." *Feminist Legal Studies* 19: 119–132.

Allen, Mike, and Alan Cooperman. 2004. "Bush Backs Amendment Banning Gay Marriage." *The Washington Post*, February 25.

Barnett, Randy. 2017. "Out of Touch Law Professor Criticizes Judge Gorsuch and Originalism." *The Washington Post*, February 25. https://www.washingtonpost.com/news/volokh-conspiracy/wp/2017/02/25/out-of-touch-law-professor-criticizes-judge-gorsuch-and-originalism/.

Boylan, Jennifer Finney. 2018. "Is America Growing Less Tolerant on L.G.B.T.Q. Rights?" *The New York Times*, January 29. https://www.nytimes.com/2018/01/29/opinion/america-tolerant-lgbtq-rights.html?rref=collection%2Ftimestopic%2FBoylan%2C%20Jennifer%20Finney&action=click&contentCollection=opinion&region=stream&module=stream_unit&version=latest&contentPlacement=3&pgtype=collection.

Brake, Elizabeth. 2012. *Minimizing Marriage: Marriage, Morality and the Law*. Oxford, UK: Oxford University Press.

Brown, Susan L. 2004. "Family Structure and Child Well-Being: The Significance of Parental Cohabitation." *Journal of Marriage and Family* 66: 351–367.

Brown, Wendy. 2004. "After Marriage." In *Just Marriage*, edited by Mary Lyndon Shanley. New York: Oxford University Press.

Brownstein, Alan E. 2015. "Perception and Reality." *Liberty Magazine*. http://www.libertymagazine.org/article/perception-and-reality.

Bush, George W. 2004. "The State of the Union." https://georgewbush-whitehouse.archives.gov/stateoftheunion/2004/.

Bybee, Keith J. 2005. "The Polite Thing to Do." In *The Future of Gay Rights in America*, edited by H.N. Hirsch. New York: Routledge.

———. 2010. *All Judges Are Political-Except When They Are Not: Acceptable Hypocrisies and the Rule of Law*. Palo Alto, CA: Stanford University Press.

Bybee, Keith J., and Cyril Ghosh. 2009. "Managing Radical Disputes: Public Reason, the American Dream, and the Case of Same-Sex Marriage." *Studies in Law, Politics and Society* 49: 125–156.

Campos, Paul F. 1994. "Secular Fundamentalism." *Columbia Law Review* 94: 1814–1827.

Chambers, Clare. 2013. "The Marriage-Free State." In *Proceedings of the Aristotelian Society* 113 (2_pt_2): 123–143.

Cook, Lindsey. 2015. "For Richer, Not Poorer: Marriage and the Growing Class Divide." *U.S. News and World Report*, October 26. https://www.usnews.com/news/blogs/datamine,2015/10/26/marriage-and-the-growing-class-divde.

Cott, Nancy F. 1998. "Marriage and Women's Citizenship in the United States, 1830–1934." *The American Historical Review* 103 (5): 1440–1474.

Defense of Marriage Act. 1996. https://www.gpo.gov/fdsys/pkg/BILLS-104hr3396enr/pdf/BILLS-104hr3396enr.pdf.

Delgado, Richard, and Jean Stefancic. 2001. *Critical Race Theory: An Introduction*. New York: New York University Press.

Department of Justice. 2012. "Interim Decision: Matter of Petersen: In Visa Petition Proceedings." https://www.justice.gov/sites/default/files/eoir/legacy/2012/08/27/1373.pdf.

DePaulo, Bella M. 2007. *Singled Out: How Singles Are Stereotyped, Stigmatized and Ignored and Still Live Happily Everafter*. New York: St. Martin's Griffin.

DePaulo, Bella M., and Wendy L. Morris. 2005. "Singles in Society and in Science." *Psychological Inquiry* 16 (2/3): 57–83.

Duggan, Lisa. 2002. "The New Homonormativity: The Sexual Politics of Neoliberalism." In *Materializing Democracy: Toward a Revitalized Cultural Politics*, edited by Russ Castronovo and Dana Nelson, 175–194. Durham, NC: Duke University Press.

Ettelbrick, Paula L. 1992. "Since When Is Marriage the Path to Liberation?" In *Lesbian and Gay Marriage: Private Commitments, Public Ceremonies*, edited by Suzanne Sherman, 20–26. Philadelphia: Temple University Press.

Ettelbrick, Paula L., and Julie Shapiro. 2004. "Are We on the Path to Liberation Now?: Same-Sex Marriage at Home and Abroad." *Seattle Journal for Social Justice* 2: 475–493.

Fish, Stanley. 1994. *There's No Such Thing as Free Speech, And It's a Good Thing Too*. New York: Oxford University Press.

———. 1997a. "Boutique Multiculturalism, or Why Liberals Are Incapable of Thinking About Hate Speech." *Critical Inquiry* 23: 378–395.

———. 1997b. "Mission Impossible: Setting the Just Bounds between Church and State." *Columbia Law Review* 97 (December): 2255–2333.

Fleming, James, and Linda McClain. 2013. *Ordered Liberty: Rights, Responsibilities, Virtues*. Cambridge, MA: Harvard University Press.

Ford, Matt. 2014. "Why the Supreme Court May Have to Rule on Gay Marriage." *The Atlantic*, November 7. http://www.theatlantic.com/politics/archive/2014/11/federal-appeals-court-upholds-same-sex-marriage-ban/382481/.

Franke, Katherine. 2009. "Theorizing Yes: An Essay on Feminism, Law and Desire." In *Feminist and Queer Legal Theory: Intimate Encounters, Uncomfortable Conversations*, edited by Martha Albertson Fineman, Jack E. Jackson, and Adam P. Romero, 29–44. New York: Routledge.

———. 2011. "Marriage Is a Mixed Blessing." *The New York Times*, June 23.

Fraser, Nancy. 1995. "From Redistribution to Recognition: Dilemmas of Justice in a 'Postsocialist' Age." *New Left Review* 1 (212 July–August): 68–93.

Freeman, Samuel. 2004. "Public Reason and Political Justifications." *Fordham Law Review* 72 (5): 2021–2072.

Frohock, Fred. 2006a. "An Alternative Model of Political Reasoning." *Ethical Theory and Moral Practice* 9: 27–64.

———. 2006b. *Bounded Divinities: Sacred Discourses in Pluralist Democracies.* New York: Palgrave Macmillan.

George, Robert P. 1997. "Public Reason and Political Conflict: Abortion and Homosexuality." *The Yale Law Journal* 106: 2475–2504.

Gerstel, Naomi, and Natalia Sarkisian. 2006. "Marriage: The Good, the Bad and the Greedy." *Contexts* 5 (4): 16–21.

Gerstmann, Evan. 2008. *Same-Sex Marriage and the Constitution*, 2nd ed. New York: Cambridge University Press.

Ghosh, Cyril. 2013. *The Politics of the American Dream: Democratic Inclusion in Contemporary American Political Culture.* New York: Palgrave Macmillan.

———. 2016. "Queer International Relations (1v): Queer as Method." *The Disorder of Things* (blog), November 24. https://thedisorderofthings.com/2016/11/24/queer-international-relations-iv-queer-as-method/.

———. 2017. "The Emergence of Marriage Equality and the Sad Demise of Civil Unions." *Studies in Law, Politics and Society* 73: 1–20.

———. 2018, forthcoming. "Marriage, Equality and the Injunction to Assimilate: Romantic Love, Children, Monogamy and Parenting in Obergefell v. Hodges." *Polity.*

Ginsberg, Ruth Bader. 1985. "Some Thoughts on Autonomy and Equality in Relation to Roe v. Wade." *North Carolina Law Review* 63: 375–386.

Gutmann, Amy, and Dennis Thompson. 1998. *Democracy and Disagreement.* Cambridge, MA: Belknap Press.

Hawkins, Alan J., Betsy Vandenberghe, and Lynae Barlow. 2017. "The New Math of Consensual Nonmonogamy." *National Review*, December 5. http://www.nationalreview.com/article/454355/consensual-non-monogamy-bad-math.

Henion, Andy, and Ann Marie Ryan. 2013. "Wanted: A Life Outside the Workplace." *MSU Today*, February 21. http://msutoday.msu.edu/news/2013/wanted-a-life-outside-the-workplace/.

Hoffman, Jan. 2016. "Gay and Lesbian High School Students Report 'Heartbreaking' Levels of Violence." *The New York Times*, August 11. https://www.nytimes.com/2016/08/12/health/gay-lesbian-teenagers-violence.html?_r=0.

Holmes, Oliver Wendell. 1897. "The Path of the Law." *Harvard Law Review* 10: 457.

Ireland, Roderick L. 2010. "In Goodridge's Wake: Reflections on the Political, Public and Personal Repercussions of the Massachusetts Same-Sex Marriage Cases." *NYU Law Review* 85 (5): 1417–1443.

Josephson, Jyl. 2005. "Citizenship, Same-Sex Marriage and Feminist Critiques of Marriage." *Perspectives on Politics* 3 (2): 269–284.

Keeney, Jessica et al. 2013. "From 'Work-Family' to 'Work-Life': Broadening Our Conceptualization and Measurement." *Journal of Vocational Behavior* 82 (3 June): 155–266.

Kennedy, Anthony. 2015. Obergefell v. Hodges.

Kinsley, Michael. 2003. "Abolish Marriage." *Washington Post*, July 3, sec. A23.

Larmore, Charles. 2002. "Public Reason." In *The Cambridge Companion to Rawls*, edited by Samuel Freeman, 368–393. New York: Cambridge University Press.

M., S. 2017. "Democracy in America: Can A Baker Refuse to Make A Gay Wedding Cake?" *The Economist*, July 7. https://www.economist.com/blogs/democracyinamerica/2017/07/just-desserts.

Macedo, Stephen. 2015. *Just Married: Same-Sex Marriage, Monogamy, and The Future of Marriage*. Princeton, NJ: Princeton University Press.

March, Andrew. 2010. "Civil Unions for All! Why the Government Should Get Out of the 'Marriage' Business." *The Huffington Post*, September 13. http://www.huffingtonpost.com/andrew-f-march/civil-unions-for-all-why-b-711858.html.

Martel, James. 2001. *Love Is a Sweet Chain: Desire, Autonomy, and Friendship in Liberal Political Theory*. New York: Routledge.

Marx, Karl. 1978. "The Eighteenth Brumaire of Louis Bonaparte." In *The Marx-Engels Reader*, 2nd ed., edited by Robert C. Tucker. New York: W.W. Norton.

Metz, Tamara. 2004. "Why We Should Disestablish Marriage." In *Just Marriage*, edited by Mary Lyndon Shanley. New York: Oxford University Press.

———. 2010. *Untying the Knot: Marriage, the State and the Case for Their Divorce*. Princeton, NJ: Princeton University Press.

Morris, Wendy L., Bella M. DePaulo, Janina Hertel, and Lindsay C. Taylor. 2008. "Singlism-Another Problem That Has No Name: Prejudice, Stereotypes and Discrimination against Singles." In *The Psychology of Modern Prejudice*, edited by Melanie A. Morrison and Todd G. Morrison, 165–194. Hauppauge, NY: Nova Science.

National Public Radio. 2017. "Religious Conservatives and Pro-Business Republicans Split Over Texas 'Bathroom Bill'." http://www.npr.org/2017/02/23/516787771/religious-conservatives-and-pro-business-republicans-split-over-texas-bathroom-b.

Owen, J. Judd. 2001. *Religion and the Demise of Liberal Rationalism: The Foundational Crisis of the Separation of Church and State.* Chicago: University of Chicago Press.

Pateman, Carole. 1988. *The Sexual Contract.* Palo Alto, CA: Stanford University Press.

Patten, Alan. 2003. "Liberal Neutrality and Language Policy." *Philosophy and Public Affairs* 31 (4): 356–386.

Perry, Keith. 2014. "Marriage Becoming 'Preserve of the Wealthy'." *Telegraph*, November 12. http://www.telegraph.co.uk/finance/11227574/marriage-becoming-preserve-of-the-wealthy.html.

Posner, Richard A. 2003. *Law, Pragmatism, and Democracy.* Cambridge, MA: Harvard University Press.

Puar, Jasbir. 2006. "Mapping US Homonormativities." *Gender, Place and Culture: A Journal of Feminist Geography* 13 (1): 67–88.

Rampell, Catherine. 2012. "Marriage Is for Rich People." *New York Times*, February 6. https://economix.blogs.nytimes.com/2012/02/06/marriage-is-for-rich-people/?_r=0.

Rawls, John. 1996. *Political Liberalism.* New York: Columbia University Press.

———. 1997. "The Idea of Public Reason Revisited." *The University of Chicago Law Review* 64 (3): 765–807.

Rosen, Jeffrey. 2006. *The Most Democratic Branch: How The Courts Serve America.* New York: Oxford University Press.

Scalia, Antonin. 1997. *A Matter of Interpretation: Federal Courts and the Law.* Princeton, NJ: Princeton University Press.

Scalia, Antonin. 2015. Obergefell v. Hodges.

Schachter, Harvey. 2013. "Who Gets to Leave Early at Your Work? Parents Only?" *The Globe and Mail*, March 21. http://www.theglobeandmail.com/report-on-business/careers/career-advice/life-at-work/who-gets-to-leave-early-at-your-work-parents-only/article10057573/.

Smith, Catherine E., Lauren Fontana, Susannah William Pollvogt, and Tanya Washington. 2015. "Brief of Amici Curiae Scholars of the Constitutional Rights of Children in Support of Petitioners in Obergefell v. Hodges." *Denver Law Review.* https://digitalcommons.du.edu/cgi/viewcontent.cgi?article=1029&context=law_facpub.

Somin, Ilya. 2015. "A Great Decision on Same-Sex Marriage – But Based on Dubious Reasoning." *Washington Post*, June 26. https://www.washingtonpost.com/news/volokh-conspiracy/wp/2015/06/26/a-great-decision-on-same-sex-marriage-but-based-on-dubious-reasoning/?utm_term=.61b032fbf403.

Stern, Mark Joseph. 2015. "Kennedy's Marriage Equality Decision Is Gorgeous, Heartfelt, and a Little Mystifying." *Slate*, June 26. http://www.slate.com/articles/news_and_politics/the_breakfast_table/features/2015/scotus_roundup/supreme_court_2015_decoding_anthony_kennedy_s_gay_marriage_decision.html.

Stone, Geoffrey R. 2015. "Supreme Court Will Rule for Marriage: Here's The Best Way," April 27. https://www.thedailybeast.com/supreme-court-will-rule-for-marriage-heres-the-best-way.

Sunstein, Cass. 1993. "Liberal Constitutionalism and Liberal Justice." *Texas Law Review* 72: 305–313.

———. 1994. "Incompletely Theorized Agreements Commentary." *Harvard Law Review* 108: 1733–1772.

———. 1996. *Legal Reasoning and Political Conflict*. New York: Oxford University Press.

———. 1999. *One Case at a Time: Judicial Minimalism on the Supreme Court*. Cambridge, MA: Harvard University Press.

Tharoor, Shashi. 1999. "Are Human Rights Universal?" *World Policy Journal* 16 (4 Winter). http://www.worldpolicy.org/tharoor.html.

Tribe, Laurence. 2015. "Equal Dignity: Speaking Its Name." *Harvard Law Review* 129: 16–32.

Trotta, Daniel. 2017. "Trump Revokes Obama Guidelines on Transgender Bathrooms." *Reuters*, February 23. https://www.reuters.com/article/us-usa-trump-lgbt-idUSKBN161243.

United Nations. 1948. "The Universal Declaration of Human Rights." http://www.un.org/en/universal-declaration-human-rights/.

United States House of Representatives. 1996. "House Report: 104–664." *Government Publishing Office*. 104th Congress. Available at: https://www.gpo.gov/fdsys/pkg/CRPT-104hrpt664/html/CRPT-104hrpt664.htm.

Warner, Michael. 1999. *The Trouble with Normal: Sex, Politics and the Ethics of Queer Life*, 2nd ed. New York: Free Press.

Warren, Earl. 1967. *Loving v. Virginia*.

Weber, Cynthia. 2016. *Queer International Relations: Sovereignty, Sexuality and the Will to Knowledge*. New York: Oxford University Press.

X, Gracie. 2015. "6 Varieties of Ethical Non-Monogamy." *The Huffington Post*, April 15, 2015. https://www.huffingtonpost.com/gracie-x/6-varieties-of-ethical-non-monogamy_b_7066490.html.

Yoshino, Kenji. 2002. "Covering." *The Yale Law Journal* 111 (4): 769–939.

———. 2015. "The Supreme Court, 2014 Term–Comment: A New Birth of Freedom?" *Harvard Law Review* 129: 77–85.

Young, Iris Marion. 1990. *Justice and the Politics of Difference*. Princeton, NJ: Princeton University Press.

Zimmerman, Augusto. 2015. "Judicial Activism and Arbitrary Control: A Critical Analysis of Obergefell v Hodges 556 [sic] US (2015)—The US Supreme Court Same-Sex Marriage Case." *The University of Notre Dame Australia Law Review* 17 (December): 77–85.

Zivi, Karen. 2014. "Performing the Nation: Contesting Same-Sex Marriage Rights in the United States." *Journal of Human Rights* 13 (September): 290–306.

CHAPTER 4

Covering's Other Hidden Assault

Abstract In this chapter, I engage with the concept of gay "covering"—as theorized by Kenji Yoshino. Gay covering refers to actions of gay and lesbian individuals to "disattend," or tone down, their (despised) sexuality in an effort to fit into and be accepted by the mainstream. In Yoshino's telling, this is the newest iteration of a set of societal (and even legal) injunctions imposed on gays and lesbians, following a sequence, in the beginning, to convert, then, to pass, and finally, to cover. I argue here that while Yoshino's analysis offers several critical insights it nonetheless elides any critical engagement with the question of agency on the part of the subject of covering. Consequently, he misunderstands the plural motivations that may lead an individual to cover. Yoshino also misreads some forms of conduct as if they encode acts of covering when in fact the individuals performing those acts are potentially merely "being themselves." Thus, Yoshino's critique ends up being just as oppressive as the oppression it is mobilized to dismantle in that it is an injunction to reverse cover. Consequently, it can harm, rather than help, LGBT+persons and curtail, rather than enhance, their freedoms.

Keywords "acting straight" · "acting white" · Civil rights · Covering
Stigma

C. Ghosh, *De-Moralizing Gay Rights*,
https://doi.org/10.1007/978-3-319-78840-1_4

4.1 Introduction

Kenji Yoshino has theorized the idea of "covering" in the context of civil rights. His first major treatment of the idea appears in a *Yale Law Journal* piece, "Covering" (Yoshino 2002). Subsequently, he expanded the argument into a book, *Covering: The Hidden Assault on Our Civil Rights* (Yoshino 2006). Yoshino engages with the covering phenomenon in the race-based, sex-based, and sexual orientation-based contexts. In each, Yoshino attempts to describe how the injunction to cover functions in the domain of the law as well as that of culture.

The concept of covering, we learn from Yoshino, can be traced back to Erving Goffman, who, in his 1963 work, *Stigma: Notes on the Management of Spoiled Identity*, described it as a phenomenon that occurs when "persons who are ready to admit possession of a stigma...may nonetheless make a great effort to keep the stigma from looming large" (Goffman, quoted in Yoshino [2002, 772]). As Yoshino describes it, gay covering occurs, for example, when a person who identifies as lesbian reveals to the people around her (at work or at a social gathering) that she identifies as such and then proceeds to make it easy for the same audience to "disattend her orientation" (Yoshino 2002, 772). She may do so, for example, by making sure she does absolutely nothing to remind them that she is someone who sexually desires a person of the same sex. In this effort, she may, for example, "(1) not engage in public displays of same-sex affection; (2) not engage in gender-atypical activity that could code as gay; or (3) not engage in gay activism" (Yoshino 2002, 772).

To cover, then, is to do the opposite of "flaunting" or "signaling" (Yoshino 2002, 776, *passim*). Yoshino is interested in tracing the lineaments of the pressures placed on marginal groups—like sexual orientation and racial minorities and women—to engage in this conduct, to cover their *difference* (Young 1990; Fraser 1995, 1997; Ghosh 2013, especially 67–72). In the legal context, in particular, Yoshino demonstrates how, in judgment after judgment, courts have imposed the demand to cover on gays, racial minorities, and women and penalized them for flaunting their difference. In the civil service and custody and visitation contexts, for example, gays and lesbians have been routinely asked to cover by the courts—or asked to deemphasize their LGBT+ identity in their behavior/conduct.

Yoshino is also interested in proposing an antidiscrimination paradigm that seeks to permanently alter this landscape of civil rights jurisprudence in the United States. He begins "Covering" (2002) by identifying the pressures that gay people, particularly gay men, have historically experienced in the US, first, to convert, and then to pass, and finally, to cover. Having traced this evolution, he then focuses on demonstrating how gay covering functions in the cultural context. He then analogizes the phenomenon of gay covering to the way covering functions in the context of race and sex/gender. It turns out that the injunction to cover presents itself in all sorts of civil rights contexts. Thus, for example, in the legal context of race-based covering, Yoshino draws from case law related to grooming and language policies and demonstrates how racial minorities are routinely asked to cover by the state as it compels people of color to assimilate into white and Anglo-Saxon norms.

Equally, in the legal context of sex-based covering, Yoshino discusses sex discrimination cases related to pregnancy, demeanor, and grooming, to show how women are routinely both asked to cover and asked to—as he terms it—"reverse cover" (see, for example, Yoshino 2002, 780, 781, 871). Reverse covering, in Yoshino's characterization, does not exclusively happen in the context of sex-based covering, but it is germane to it, and occurs, for example, when women are pressured into conducting themselves in ways that more closely align with what is socially coded as "feminine" behavior (Yoshino 2002, 780, *passim*).

The discussions of these three legal contexts is a major—indeed paradigm-shifting—critical intervention and will in all likelihood change the substantive nature of, and public discourse on, civil rights jurisprudence in the US at some point in the foreseeable future. Yoshino has single-handedly done more to erode the force of the assimilationist injunctions emanating from the federal judiciary in civil rights cases than any other legal scholar writing today.

However, notwithstanding the "hidden assault" (Yoshino 2006) on civil rights that Yoshino uncovers, there is another hidden assault embedded in the very theorization of covering that Yoshino himself advances. It is mobilized through a series of false dichotomies, each predicated on a will to shame. These binary logics reassert the very injunction to "reverse cover" that Yoshino is committed to dismantling. In the remainder of this chapter, I develop this critique. In doing so, I focus primarily on the cultural context of "gay covering." Thus, in Sect. 4.2, I begin by describing what Yoshino acknowledges as the "being themselves" critique of his work, which suggests, in effect, that Yoshino imposes his own reverse covering demand even as he disavows the practice. I also describe here what Yoshino offers as his defense in the face of this critique. As I then elaborate in Sect. 4.3, the defense Yoshino offers directly contradicts what he actually *writes*, and is, therefore, no defense at all. His written words do, as a matter of fact, amount to a call to reverse cover for gays and, in so doing, to in fact assimilate—albeit not into the mainstream but, just as oppressively, into a specific subculture.

4.2 "Being Themselves"

Close to the end of *Covering* (Yoshino 2006), on pages 189–190, Yoshino recounts what he calls a "powerful" critique of his work in "Covering" and *Covering*. This critique can be called, for simplicity's sake, the "being themselves" critique. In it, Yoshino tells us about a female colleague who resists his depiction of the covering concept in a way that can be summed up thus:

> I've touched on the problem that the covering concept might assume too quickly that individuals behaving in "mainstream" ways are hiding some true identity, when in fact they might just be "being themselves." (Yoshino 2006, 189)

Yoshino's interlocutor suggests, for example, that when she fixes her bike she is not necessarily downplaying the fact that she is a woman. She might just be fixing her bike "because it's broken" (Yoshino 2006, 190).[1] Another example she offers is that of an African-American man she knew in graduate school who studied German Romantic poetry, not because he was trying to "act white" but because he was "seized by it" (Yoshino 2006, 190). Finally, in what Yoshino calls a "*coup de grâce*," she says that, if every time minorities break stereotypes people assume they are covering some essential stereotypical identity, the stereotypes "will never go away" (Yoshino 2006, 190).

Yoshino makes an effort to address this concern. Thus, in his discussion of an African-American dean at Harvard, Yoshino says, he saw "covering at work" (Yoshino 2006, 22). But, even though this Dean's "demeanor was more patrician than any Boston Brahmin's" (Yoshino 2006, 22), Yoshino admits that this Dean may just have been "being himself, and if that was the case, [Yoshino] would be the last to press him toward more stereotypically African-American behavior" (Yoshino 2006, 23). Yoshino also suggests "that *we must not* assume that individuals behaving in "mainstream" ways are necessarily covering" (Yoshino 2006, 190, emphasis mine).

In other parts of his writing, however, Yoshino appears to shift ground. Here, he tells us that his real concern is not so much with covering *per se*, but instead with "coerced assimilation" (Yoshino 2002, 781; 2006, 26) demands. This sounds fairly reasonable until we find him changing his mind again. This time he declares that it is also not the case that he is against "all coerced covering" (Yoshino 2006, 93). Instead, he is actually only against "coerced covering that has no justification" (Yoshino 2006, 93). He also clarifies, elsewhere, that while he is opposed to covering demands he is also equally opposed to demands that individuals "reverse cover" (Yoshino 2006, 190). Obviously, Yoshino protests too much. As I describe in the next section, Yoshino's theory of covering itself slips in and out of demands to reverse cover and this is particularly true of his discussion of gay covering in the cultural context. It is to this analysis that I now turn.

4.3 Only One Way to Be Gay

Despite Yoshino's best efforts, the concept of "gay covering" (in the cultural context) that he wishes to theorize ultimately comes across as proposing an assimilationist demand of its own. This is not to say that gays and lesbians are never coerced into covering. Some undoubtedly are. But instead it is to say that Yoshino is unable to develop the concept here as a theory that can be disaggregated from its own moralizing and sanctimonious injunction to reverse cover, and therefore to assimilate, albeit not into the mainstream but instead into a subcultural norm. The way this plays out in the text is through a trope of "acting straight" mobilized throughout it in order to recommend a reverse covering regimen and indeed demanding the "flaunting" of one's homosexuality or otherwise non-normative sexual orientation/gender identity.

In addition, Yoshino's pronouncements about *a* gay "culture" are considerably more problematic than it appears at first. Its deeply ingrained racial and class bias—and its apparent agnosticism (even as Yoshino mentions the concept) about intersectionality (Yoshino 2002, 780; see also Crenshaw 1991)—end up reenacting the same kind of violence that his critiques are intended to disassemble and unsettle. Those with cross-cutting, and intersecting, identities may only partially, or not at all, recognize themselves in the gay cultural context that Yoshino so effortlessly takes for granted as the norm for all gays and lesbians (but particularly gay men) to affiliate with and into.

Yoshino also deploys a shaming strategy based on the charge that some gay men engage in conduct that might be read as "acting straight." This is a version of the canard of "acting white."[2] But, to be sure, Yoshino appears hesitant about using the phrase itself. This may be because he is uncertain about explicitly leveling this charge. Or it may be because he is genuinely confused about how to phrase his critique. We cannot know what causes this hesitation. What we do know, however, is that this uncertainty is much more apparent in "Covering" than in *Covering*. In the former, the phrase "acting straight" is used only once. And that too in the "passing" context, where it is not used with the same illocutionary force, as I show below, as "acting white." In *Covering*, however, he uses the phrase with much less reluctance.

In "Covering," the hesitations result in some ambiguity about whether the phrase/term belongs within the category of "passing," or of "covering," or both. Thus, on the one hand, Yoshino says the "straight-acting homosexual" [observe, carefully, *not* a homosexual who is "acting straight," but instead a "straight-acting" homosexual] is a central character of the covering context:

> Gays can cover by suggesting that their gender of object choice is the only way in which they are gender atypical…Thus, gays who seek to downplay their orientation can often effectively do so by conforming to stereotypes about their gender. This is the force of the "*straight-acting*" homosexual… (Yoshino 2002, 843–844, emphasis mine)

On the other hand, "acting straight" is also what one is doing when one is passing, when Yoshino says, for example, that:

> Passing is *acting straight* by feigning an interest in sports, by creating a fictitious girlfriend, by laughing at the right jokes… (Yoshino 2002, 812, emphasis mine)

It behooves us to pause here and consider what the words "straight-acting" and the words "acting straight" mean in these two excerpts and if there are any differences between the two. Upon reflection, it turns out, that the two phrases, even though they share family resemblances, do not, after all, advance the same claims. The word "acting" in the phrase "acting straight," used here in the passing context, is actually being used *literally*. Those who are passing as straight are, in fact, *acting* as if they are straight when they know very well that they are not. Their intended audience consists of people who are not supposed to know, if these individuals can help it, that they are gay. The phrase, as it is used here, does not at all have the same illocutionary force as the phrase "acting white" does in the race-based covering context—which is a call to shame racial minorities into behavior that more stereotypically codes as non-white.

For, if the phrase "acting straight" were to be deployed with the same illocutionary force as the phrase "acting white," then two things would have to be true. First, no reasonable person could think that these individuals are, in fact, straight, just as in the racial context nobody thinks that the individual being accused of "acting white" is, in fact, white. Thus, if these individuals are, in fact, passing, then they are not "acting straight" in the same way as one "acts" white. And second, no reasonable person could think that the person leveling the charge of "acting straight" is endorsing the practice, as in the racial context nobody thinks that an individual is being applauded when they are being told that they are "acting white." In fact, the critique is intended as a demand: the demand to change one's behavior and make it conform to the conduct usually performed by, and associated with, one's ilk.

The latter is indeed happening here (arguably), in this "passing" context, but the former is not. Therefore, the phrase "acting straight," even though it phonetically resonates with the term "acting white," is in fact being deployed relatively benignly here. But both of these criteria—not-passing *and* non-endorsement—are met in the use of the phrase "straight-acting homosexual" in the covering context quoted above, and where it is underwritten by the full force of Yoshino's moralizing disapproval. It meets the first criterion because the "straight-acting homosexual" in the covering context is, after all, not passing. And it meets the second criterion because the charge of "straight-acting homosexual" is intended here as a demand to change one's conduct. In other words, it is a demand to reverse cover: homosexuals should not be straight-acting; instead, we should all be gay-acting (whatever that entails). Thus, here, although the literal phrase being used is "straight-acting" as opposed to "acting straight," its illocutionary force is the same as the phrase "acting white."

The specific injunctions against "straight-acting" behavior are also predicated on a series of false dichotomies about conduct or "performativities," (see, especially, Yoshino 2002, 865–875), as Yoshino, channeling Butler, chooses to call them. Depending on how you behave in relation to these dichotomies, you are either engaged in gay signaling or you are engaged in gay covering. No theoretical justification is ever provided for why these dichotomies are useful heuristic tools that help to clarify what the concept is meant to represent. Instead, they are simply declared in an "exemplary rather than an exhaustive spirit" (Yoshino 2002, 842). But it is important for us to note that they are declared not without a purpose. Instead, these declarations are employed in service of a series of judgments that issue from Yoshino's determinations about where any given individual finds themselves in relation to a (pre)scribed list of ways in which gays can either signal or cover.

Thus, according to Yoshino, in "Covering," some axes along which "gays can cover"[3] are:

- Abstention from Sodomy vs. Engagement in Sodomy;
- Private Displays of Same-Sex Affection vs. Public Displays;
- Gender Typical vs. Gender Atypical;
- Straight Culture Focused vs. Gay Culture Focused;
- Nonactivist vs. Activist;
- Prioritizing Other Identities vs. Prioritizing Gay Identity;
- Allied with Straights vs. Allied with Other Gays;
- Allied with the Mainstream vs. Allied with Other "Deviants" [polygamists, pedophiles, etc.];
- Monogamous vs. Promiscuous;
- Single or Secretly Coupled vs. Openly Coupled;

Limitations on space compel me to be selective. So, I have decided to engage below with three paradigmatic axes from this list. These are: "Abstention from Sodomy vs. Engagement in Sodomy;" "Gender Typical vs. Gender Atypical;" and "Straight Culture Focused vs. Gay Culture Focused."

4.3.1 *Abstention from Sodomy vs. Engagement in Sodomy*

First, let's examine what is meant by "Abstention from Sodomy vs. Engagement in Sodomy." We are told that "perhaps the most fundamental way in which gays can cover" is by abstaining from sodomy. The word sodomy is here intended to mean: "any sexual activity between individuals of the same sex" (Yoshino 2002, 842). Observe that, in this characterization, the refusal to engage in sodomy *may* be an act of covering ("perhaps the most fundamental way in which gays *can* cover"). However, it may not be. But we are never told what it is that needs to happen for us to make the decision that any specific gay man's[4] abstention from sodomy is, indeed, motivated by a desire to cover. The canonical example of this kind of abstention-related covering demand Yoshino cites is the military's (erstwhile) "Don't Ask, Don't Tell" policy, which used to posit that one could be gay and serve in the military as long as one did not self-identify as such and engage in homosexual sodomy.[5]

The example sounds perfectly fine until one realizes that this discussion does not belong here. The section of the article where this discussion appears is demarcated as one in which *cultural* demands to cover are being discussed. The legal demand to cover in the orientation-based context is supposedly discussed in a separate section. In spite of this, the reader is being presented here with an example of a *statutory* demand for gay covering as a paradigmatic case of a *cultural* demand for it. No concrete example of a cultural covering demand (that reasonable people can agree as being, in fact, a cultural covering demand) to abstain from sodomy is ever provided.

Nor is it sufficiently acknowledged that not all instances of voluntary celibacy constitute covering. Is it possible that a person who is not engaged in sodomy is *being themselves*? For example, in a free society, a gay man is entitled, surely, if he so wishes, to have sexual intimacy exclusively with a romantic partner, like some—but by no means all—straight people do. And he is entitled to remain celibate during those periods when that romantic partnership is proving to be elusive. (Yes, some, but not all, straight people also do this.) But not having casual sex when one is looking for love is not necessarily covering, as Yoshino so misleadingly suggests, when he says, here and elsewhere, that sodomy might actually *constitute* gay "status" (Yoshino 2002, 866).

The full implication of Yoshino's analysis here is this: one must be engaged in intimate sexual contact with another person of the same sex before one can legitimately self-identify as a gay person who does not cover. Celibacy/abstention is not really an option: all contrary viewpoints have been exiled through the simple act of asserting the false dichotomy: abstention vs. engagement.

But this "reverse covering" injunction will not stand up to the most rudimentary scrutiny. How frequently, one might ask, does a gay man need to engage in homosexual sodomy to pass Yoshino's reverse covering muster? Can one take little breaks during which they are celibate?

How long of such a break is too long? Is one week of celibacy too long? Is one day? And so on and so forth.

4.3.2 *Gender Typical vs. Gender Atypical*

A demand to "reverse cover" is also central to the dichotomy presented as "Gender Typical vs. Gender Atypical." We know we are going to encounter some problems here right off the bat because the rubric itself—"gender typical vs. gender atypical"—appears to be an attempt to stabilize gender performances into two concrete species, one that is being called typical and one that is being called atypical. But it is already widely known, post-Butler (Butler 1990, 2004)—whom Yoshino has carefully read (see, especially, Yoshino 2002, 865–875)—that both materiality and performativity govern the presentation of, regulation of, consumption of, and indeed literacy and linguistic uptake regarding, gender. We also know, from Butler, that gender is about norms that get produced by itself, and its own repetition, while also itself being the possible locus of its own deconstruction and indeed self-destruction. Gender, therefore, is an always already unstable category: it is about normalization as well as deconstruction. Given these facts about gender, any announcement that attempts to classify (and indeed ossify) gender-related conduct into stable categories seems *prima facie* suspect even before one has read what Yoshino has to say as an elaboration of the offending rubric.[6] And when he does in fact elaborate on the theme, one of the central claims is this:

> Effeminate men and masculine women are often assumed to be homosexual, suggesting that gender and orientation are bundled in popular consciousness — to be gender atypical is to be orientation atypical and vice versa. (Yoshino 2002, 844)

There are two propositions here. The first is a relatively unproblematic claim, one that posits that gender and orientation are bundled in popular consciousness. This is, of course, widely known. Effeminate men and masculine women are indeed routinely assumed to be gay and lesbian, respectively. The second proposition here, however, is a slightly more controversial one in that it attempts to establish a link between gender atypicality and orientation atypicality.

One would have no problems with this claim if it was, in fact, true beyond a reasonable doubt. But it is not. To begin with, when Yoshino makes the claim (excerpted above), he offers a citation as evidence. But it is never absolutely clear if the citation is supposed to offer evidence for the first proposition in the sentence or the second one. One can, however, make the inference that it is being offered as evidence for the first proposition. There are two reasons for this. First, this citation is to Francisco Valdes's essay, "Queers, Sissies, Dykes and Tomboys: Deconstructing the Conflation of "Sex," "Gender," and "Sexual Orientation" in Euro-American Law and Society" (Valdes 1995). It is already a sign that this piece cannot be evidence for the second claim because the very title of the citation appears to make a strong case *against—and not for*—drawing an association between gender and sexual orientation, which is, just to be perfectly clear, precisely what Yoshino is doing in the second proposition.

The second reason why we can be pretty sure that the source is meant to be corroborating evidence for the first proposition is this: the text that appears in the page numbers indicated in the citation (51–55) do, actually, make the case that sexual orientation is often assumed to be related to "sex-determined gender," (Valdes 1995, 51) which happens to be the content of the first proposition.

The uncomfortable detail here, however, is that Valdes's essay then goes on to, quite vehemently, reject what Yoshino posits as his second proposition – which is that there is in fact a connection between sexual orientation and gender performance. Here is a short, but relevant, excerpt from Valdes's text itself:

> [The] conflation [of sex, gender, and sexual orientation] sustains Euro-centric hetero-patriarchal traditions and practices based on sex, gender, and sexual orientation hierarchies that especially and intentionally disfavor sexual minorities and women. (Valdes 1995, 364)

Yoshino's claim that "to be gender atypical is to be orientation atypical, and vice versa" is therefore an unsubstantiated assertion that is very much in need of supporting evidence—and also, mystifyingly, happens to be strongly refuted by the source cited at the end of the sentence that itself makes the claim. This is particularly problematic because the assertion—that gender and orientation atypicality are linked—is supposed to serve a function here as a supporting premise for a longer, more elaborate, argument. It is expected not merely to ground the claim that gender atypicality is correlated with a "gay" sexual orientation but indeed to advance the far more adventurous claim that the two are in fact co-constituted, which, in turn, is supposed to establish, as a fact, that if a gay person is performing their gender in a typical way, then, they are invariably covering—because, recall, "to be gender atypical is to be orientation atypical, and vice versa." No room here, observe, for gay men who act in a "gender typical" manner to claim that they are simply *being themselves*. Indeed, the game is rigged. Either you accept the false dichotomy, or you must be invested in endorsing covering. And we all know covering is a terrible thing.

The demand/injunction is unmistakable: if a gay person wishes to not cover along this axis, they should perform their gender in an atypical (what, by the way, are the exact constitutive elements of gender atypicality and who decides what these are?) way. In other words, these gays should, yes, reverse cover.

4.3.3 Straight Culture Focused vs. Gay Culture Focused

One of the indicators of gay covering, apparently, is a gay person's focus on straight culture. This part of the discussion is replete with a set of sweeping generalizations and indeed essentializing tropes about what constitutes gay culture. No definition-building or concept-clarification exercise is even attempted, let alone provided, regarding the word "culture."[7] Instead, the reader is simply informed about some of the constitutive elements of gay culture:

> There are gay fashions (e.g., boxer briefs, Carhharts, goatees); gay music (e.g., ABBA, difranco, lang, Madonna); gay divas (e.g., Davis, Dietrich, Garbo, Garland); gay authors (e.g., Barnes, Bishop, H.D., Proust, Wilde); gay magazines (e.g., *Martha Stewart Living*, *On Our Backs*, *Out*); gay diseases (e.g., hepatitis, HIV); gay drugs (e.g., K, poppers); gay ghettos (e.g., Chelsea, Provincetown); gay films (e.g., *But I'm a Cheerleader*, *Go Fish*); gay TV shows (e.g., *Ellen*, *Will and Grace*); gay sports (golf, gymnastics, rugby); gay operas (all of them?).

One really must ask: why is everyone mentioned here white? And where is, for example, James Baldwin? Or Langston Hughes? Or Alice Walker? Where is Slyvia Rivera? Where is Alvin Ailey? Marsha P. Johnson? Bessie Smith? Where is ballroom dancing? Where is voguing? Where is Willi Ninja? And (for heaven's sake!) where is Parveen Babi lip-synching to *jawaani janeman* at a New York City "Sholay" party?

The problem here is not so much that the icons mentioned here are overwhelmingly white. It is that *every single icon* mentioned here is white. And it is not merely that there is a class bias in this description. But that the *entire description is dripping* with classism.[8] Who actually plays golf? What on earth is rugby, and who, in fact, cares about it? Who has read Proust? And who, one really must ask, likes opera (yes, "all of them")?

What, it really behooves us to ask, is the class position of the Eternal Gay Subject of Yoshino's "gay culture"? And where has Yoshino's commitment to "intersectionality" (Yoshino 2002, 780; see also Crenshaw 1991) gone off to? Elsewhere, Yoshino signals his approving endorsement of an indictment of mainstream media's obsession with "white" gay culture, even as he, as we have seen, finally, is invested in reconstituting an image of exactly such a white (and intellectually/socioeconomically elitist) gay subculture.

Here is Yoshino, expressing his discomfort with the prioritization the white gay male experience as representative of "the gay experience" as if he is himself not complicit in this exercise at all:

> One obvious skew in current identity politics debate is an inattention to the intersectionality of identity. The "gay" experience that often makes it into the mainstream media is predominantly the white male gay experience. To protect attributes that are specifically white male gay traits as constitutive of gay identity is to ameliorate one problem while exacerbating another. (Yoshino 2002, 938)

One would think that in *Covering*, which was published about four years after "Covering" did, Yoshino would have addressed or revised some of his assertions about gay culture. But this never happens. Instead, the discussion of gay culture takes this modified form here:

> [G]ay TV shows like *The L Word* and *Will and Grace*, gay musicians like k.d. lang and Elton John, gay fashions like Carhartts and boxer briefs, gay divas like Garland and Garbo, gay authors like Barnes and Wilde, gay drugs like K and poppers, gay sports like figure skating and gymnastics. (Yoshino 2006, 83)

The major differences, here, as any reasonable person would see, is that Elton John makes an appearance (ABBA, difranco, and Madonna are out).

And figure skating has now come to replace golf and rugby. Proust, mercifully, has been unceremoniously dispensed with.

Having said all this, I must reiterate that it is easy to get mired in the objections to Yoshino's reification of "gay culture," and lose sight of the fact that these generalizations are ultimately being deployed here for a reason. We are meant to understand that gay covering occurs when gay people misrecognize these icons.[9] When one "minimizes," we are told, one's "participation in or reference to such culture icons," one ends up covering (Yoshino 2002, 845). This is, Yoshino declares, a "classic move of gay *disidentification*" (Yoshino 2002, 845, emphasis in the original).

But why should we abide by this declaration? Who identifies and who *disidentifies* with Yoshino's characterization of "gay culture"? And why do they do so? Is it because what Yoshino has posited as gay culture only resonates with a small minority of people but is nonetheless intended to stand in here as representative of the entire gay experience? You bet it is. Thus, once again we are faced with Yoshino's injunction to reverse cover. If one is gay, one has to like Provincetown, figure skating, and opera. If you don't, you are engaged in gay covering.

In a remarkable move, Yoshino, in *Covering*, sensibly moves away from any discussion of these ten axes of covering. But this time, he simply announces that he believes there are four axes of covering (Yoshino 2006, 79). (Nothing is said here about the ten axes mentioned in "Covering" in an "exemplary rather than an exhaustive" spirit.)

> [Gays] can cover along many axes. I believe there are four. *Appearance* concerns how an individual physically presents herself to the world. *Affiliation* concerns her cultural identifications. *Activism* concerns how much she politicizes her identity. *Association* concerns her choice of fellow travelers–lovers, friends, colleagues. There are the dimensions along which gays decide just how gay we want to be. (Yoshino 2006, 79, emphasis in the original)

Observe, once again, here, how agency has shifted. Gone are the days of coerced covering. Now, suddenly, we are making independent decisions about what, or how much, we cover—and in what domain. And what, or how much, we reveal—and in what domain. Thus, in this telling, we decide, insouciantly, and on our own, "just how gay we want to be." There is nary a structural pressure—or coercion, or cultural demand to cover—to be had. Once again, limitations of space preclude me from engaging with each of these discussions in greater detail. As a prototypical case, however, I critically interrogate the axis of "affiliation" below.

At the center of the discussion on affiliation-based covering, is Yoshino's engagement with Fire Island and its place in gay cultural life. He begins by saying that, for a long time, he resisted making a trip out to Fire Island because he was "afraid [his] bookish self would be out of place there, and afraid of succumbing to cliché" (Yoshino 2006, 82). This all changed, however, when he did, in fact, make a trip to Fire Island—that international stereotype of a gay mecca[10]—on New York's Long Island.

We are then told of a Fire Island "culture of sex and camp and whimsy" (Yoshino 2006, 83) that binds (some) gay people to a "community with a history and a geography" (Yoshino 2006, 83). When Yoshino first encounters this campy headiness, he is reminded of a colleague of his, who, a non-observant Jew, resisted going to Israel until adulthood and yet wanted to "kiss the earth" (Yoshino 2006, 83) upon touchdown when he did eventually make his first trip there.

Yoshino's euphoria, however, we are then told, is short-lived. The very act of leaving Fire Island also painfully represents for him the cultural covering demand that gays experience all the time. At some point during the train ride back from "the Pines" (Yoshino 2006, 85) he looks up and observes that straight culture had "reasserted itself" (Yoshino 2006, 85). Men lolling in each other's arms are now no longer sitting intertwined with each other; interlaced fingers are now disengaged.

Presumably, one is supposed to make the inference from all this, although it is nowhere explicitly stated, that not affiliating oneself with Fire Island would constitute affiliation-based gay covering. But what is not being said here is that Fire Island may not be a (perfectly reasonable) gay man's first choice as a "beach" vacation or a "gay" vacation for a range of reasons. I cite three here as examples:

First, Fire Island is quite expensive in the summer-time, which is really the only meaningful time to visit the place; some people may make the decision that their money (if they have the money to spend, in the first place) is better spent doing something else. Second, the place is really not that beautiful at all. New Zealand has much nicer beaches. So does the Mediterranean. And third, some gay men may simply reject the idea of rushing off to a space where they can *temporarily* loll in each other's arms and *temporarily* sit around with interlaced fingers—the entire time with the absolute certainty that these freedoms are carefully circumscribed and their outer boundaries taper off at some indeterminate point between Sayville and Penn Station on the Long Island Rail Road. Why, then, would Yoshino say that not affiliating oneself with Fire Island is a form of gay covering? Why can't this decision be read as some gays just "being themselves"? We, of course, do not know because Yoshino never tells us.

One remaining word must be said here: it may be the case that, for Yoshino, "Fire Island" is merely a metaphor and that reading the text literally here is inadvisable. That, maybe, Yoshino does not literally mean to imply that all gay men must affiliate themselves with Fire Island. (In "Covering," as indicated above, Yoshino talks about Provincetown and Chelsea with similar approval.)

Well, even if this were to be the case, and "Fire Island" merely serves here as a stand-in for all gay enclaves and "gayborhoods," the species of criticism suggested in my third objection above would still hold. Why must *everyone* want a freedom that they know will be taken away from them soon? We are, surely, allowed to *disaffiliate* ourselves from freedoms that come to us with an expiration date.

It is precisely this agency on the part of the queer subject that Yoshino cannot bring himself to acknowledge, confront, or engage with. When gay men *disaffiliate* from "gay culture" they may be catalyzed by a desire to be self-protective, self-affirming, politically subversive, or some combination of one or more of these motivations. They are not necessarily covering. Never interlocking their fingers with their lovers' as they sit on the Long Island Rail Road, or rejecting Fire Island altogether, might, therefore, be a way of *rejecting* the cultural demand to cover when straight culture has "reasserted itself" and not a form of capitulation to it. It need not be read mandatorily as the queer subject "acting straight." As I describe in some detail in the next and concluding section, in at least one view, reading motivation into conduct is a dangerously misguided exercise and one should proceed with extreme caution in this endeavor.

4.4 Reading Motivation

Consider, for a moment, the case of *Church of Lukumi Babalu Aye v. City of Hialeah* (1993), in which a unanimous US Supreme Court struck down a specific ordinance in the city of Hialeah. The Court found that, even though the ordinance was facially neutral in its proscription of all animal slaughter, it nonetheless violated the free exercise rights of those who followed the Santeria religion. The opinion of the Court included a discussion of the intentions of the lawmakers and the negative attitude and demeanor toward the Santeria religion (Kennedy 1993, especially, Part II-A-2) that they apparently disclosed as they deliberated about this ordinance. It concluded that the "history" (Kennedy 1993, 542) of the lawmakers' attitudes and pronouncements demonstrated that the object of the ordinances was to impermissibly "target animal sacrifice by Santeria worshippers."

Justice Scalia did not, however, join this section of the opinion, writing, instead, in a concurring opinion, in which he was joined by Chief Justice Rehnquist and Justice Thomas, that the Court should not be in the "business of invalidating laws by reason of the evil motives of their authors" (Scalia 1993, 558). Justice Scalia disagreed that the "subjective motivation" of the lawmakers could be reliably discovered. Although he did not foreclose the possibility altogether, he did say that the task was "virtually impossible" (Scalia 1993, 558).

This admonition should be taken seriously. In our daily lives, we all carelessly, and routinely, ascribe motivations in and to others. As an academic, I might say, for example, a specific compliment from a student is an instance of flattery or "sucking up to the professor." On other occasions, I might determine—without being able to sufficiently explain why—that a specific compliment strikes me as, in fact, sincere.

But it is one thing for us to do this in our ordinary, daily, lives. And quite another for the US Supreme Court to include such determinations in its judgments, especially if it is being done in the absence of overwhelming evidence to support the claim.[11] Or for someone like Yoshino to ascribe motivations to conduct in order to theorize a sociological concept.

To say this is not to say that we can never understand motivation behind conduct, or even that it is necessary to do so before we can recognize the presence of a cultural demand, such as that of covering. Nor is it to say that Yoshino's use of narratives does not have critical, or explanatory, power. The fields of Critical Legal Studies and Critical Race Theory, after all, take it, correctly, as axiomatic that narratives can sometimes achieve that which no treatise or dissertation can (see, for example, Delgado and Stefancic 2001).

Consider, in this regard, Yoshino's discussion of race-based covering. Here, he refers, for example, to Richard Delgado's observation that he (Delgado) was advised, early in his academic career, "not to write on "civil rights or other 'ethnic' subjects" prior to tenure" (Yoshino 2002,

886). He also describes how Patricia Williams, who is black, was asked by a coworker to not make "too much" of her race (Yoshino 2002, 887). Each of these vignettes is stunningly effective in mobilizing a critique. If one has a soul, even half a soul, one should at least be a little bit irritated by these awful cultural demands. Each story here can also be *reliably* interpreted to identify the specific, insidious, cultural demand to cover that is being imposed on these individuals.

Yoshino, however, rushes past these narratives, as if their analytical prowess is sufficiently leveraged merely in their *telling*. Just as he does in the gay covering context, in the race-covering context too, Yoshino finds himself much more committed to mobilizing a critique based on "shaming" the individual for "covering" than in an analysis of what, in fact, constitutes a cultural demand to race cover. Thus, he devotes swathes of text analyzing (and ascribing motivations to) the behavior of Lawrence Mungin—whose story centers around his *own decision*—and not around any cultural demand—to play the part of the "good black" (Yoshino 2002, 884). Yoshino acknowledges that Mungin explicitly says: "I wanted to show that I was like white people" (Yoshino 2002, 884). In spite of this profession, however, Yoshino apparently does not think Mungin was *being himself*, and inserts a discussion of Mungin's race covering narrative into a section of "Covering" where he is ostensibly engaged in analyzing *cultural demands* to cover. The intention here is, presumably, to demonstrate what one *should not* be doing when faced with the option to race cover.

The theorization also faces here another difficulty. Even as he critiques Mungin's decision to race cover, Yoshino mystifyingly tells us that he has himself benefited from race covering: "I have received the benefit of the social contract of racial covering…I have covered my race and moved to the center of American society" (Yoshino 2006, 130). Why, one might ask, has Yoshino elided a discussion here on why racial covering has helped him but it has not helped Mungin? Does race-based covering produce different results for Asian-Americans than it does for black Americans? (Can one even generalize about entire racial groups from these two cases?) Is there a role of class and socioeconomic status here? Are these both instances of coerced covering? And if not, why not? What is it that makes one coerced covering and the other non-coerced covering?

None of these questions is ever addressed. As a result, there is no programmatic action, or intervention, to be had, or conceptualized, as a consequence of Yoshino's critique of Mungin's race-based covering.

There is no room, in other words, to even imagine a remedy since we have not had a chance to identify the precise violation or injury. The reason for this is because Yoshino is not, finally, interested in developing a programmatic action in the cultural contexts he discusses. Nor is he interested in locating the blame for covering in those who make the cultural demands to cover. Instead, he is interested in shaming the people who, in his telling, have succumbed to these cultural demands. In so doing, he hopes he can urge them to reverse cover.

This injunction in Yoshino's theorization works, as I hope to have shown throughout this chapter, because Yoshino's narratives are presented as if they enable us to unproblematically read motivation into conduct. The critique of covering is thus mobilized on the backs of personae that we come to regard—because *we know* their motivation—as inauthentic. Thus, we end up with the figure of the celibate and/or Fire Island-hating gay male. Or with the figure of the straight-acting gay male who is always already engaged in public acts of artfully draping a shroud of masculinity over a bedrock effeminacy. But, this is not the only view to be had on this subject, as Yoshino so casually assumes. Together with Justice Scalia, we should be suspicious of this argumentative strategy and resist it on the ground that reading motivation behind conduct—in narratives or any other context—is a dangerously misguided proposition that can have the insidious effect of shaming members of vulnerable minorities for exercising a modicum of whatever agency they have.

It is possible, but not certain, that Yoshino will one day revise his work on covering and, this time, be attentive to the slippages and unreasonable injunctions to reverse cover identified throughout this chapter—both in the race-based (as briefly discussed here) and in the sexual orientation-based covering contexts. That is, in the next revision of the text, Yoshino might perhaps take seriously Justice Scalia's uncertainty about ascribing motivation to others and, as a result, strip the text of those tropes in it that seek to condemn people for *being themselves*. Let's hope that he does, indeed, one day, offer exactly such a revision.

Notes

1. For another version of this critique, also see p. 935 in "Covering": "The concern still remains that whenever a racial minority, woman, or homosexual is seen behaving in a non-stereotypical manner, she will be vulnerable to the interpretation that she is "covering"" (Yoshino 2002, 935).

2. It is well known that African-Americans in particular, but also other racial minorities, live with the widespread social expectation that their conduct must somehow signal to others that they are not too closely affiliated with "white" culture. Or else they are accused by others, from both within and without the specific racial group, of "acting white." We all know that the phrase itself will not survive the mildest lines of interrogation: what constitutes whiteness, for example? Or even white culture, for that matter? Yet, as a practical matter, this kind of "shaming" happens all the time. Even Barack and Michelle Obama have repeatedly critiqued the oppressiveness of the charge as they have opposed the view, among some members of the black community, that academic achievement is "synonymous with whiteness" (Henderson 2014).
3. The phrase "gays can cover" appears in the opening sentence of the discussion pertaining to each of the ten axes of covering. See, "Covering," (Yoshino 2002, 842–848).
4. For simplicity's sake, here, and in the remainder of this chapter, I am bracketing out other sexual orientation minorities.
5. Yoshino points out that gay identifying speech was also proscribed under "Don't Ask, Don't Tell" (Yoshino 2002, 828, 842–843; see also Lehring 2003, 2).
6. Yoshino at one point does acknowledge that his "axes" are plagued by "heuristic overschematization," which, in his estimation, is a "necessary evil" (Yoshino 2002, 780).
7. The term culture, of course, is an "essentially contested concept" (Ghosh 2013, 25). On essentially contested concepts, see, variously, Gallie (1956), Gerring (1999), Collier et al. (2006), and Cohen (2009).
8. This point is especially effectively made by Horowitz (2007, especially, 1294–1296).
9. On the concept of "misrecognition," see, variously, Young (1990) and Fraser (1995, 1997).
10. As in noted in Chapter 3, Katherine Franke uses this phrase (ironically) to talk about Tel Aviv (Franke 2012, 9).
11. To be sure, reasonable people can disagree about whether the evidence for this claim in *Lukumi* was, in fact, indubitable. Justice Scalia, for one, seemed to think it was not reliable.

References

Butler, Judith. 1990. *Gender Trouble: Feminism and the Subversion of Identity*. New York: Routledge.

———. 2004. "Gender Regulations." In *Undoing Gender*. New York: Routledge.

Cohen, Elizabeth F. 2009. *Semi-Citizenship in Democratic Politics*. New York: Cambridge University Press.

Collier, David, Daniel Hidalgo, and Andra Olivia Maciuceanu. 2006. "Essentially Contested Concepts: Debates and Applications." *Journal of Political Ideologies* 11 (3): 211–246.

Crenshaw, Kimberle. 1991. "Mapping the Margins: Intersectionality, Identity Politics, and Violence Against Women of Color." *Stanford Law Review* 43 (6): 1241–1299.

Delgado, Richard, and Jean Stefancic. 2001. *Critical Race Theory: An Introduction*. New York: New York University Press.

Franke, Katherine M. 2012. "Dating the State: The Moral Hazards of Winning Gay Rights." *Columbia Human Rights Law Review* 44 (1): 1–46.

Fraser, Nancy. 1995. "From Redistribution to Recognition: Dilemmas of Justice in a 'Postsocialist' Age." *New Left Review* 1/212 (July–August): 68–93.

———. 1997. *Justice Interruptus: Critical Reflections on the "Postsocialist" Condition*. New York: Routledge.

Gallie, Walter Bryce. 1956. "Essentially Contested Concepts." *Proceedings of the Aristotelian Society* 56: 167–198.

Gerring, John. 1999. "What Makes a Concept Good? A Criterial Framework for Understanding Concept Formation in the Social Sciences." *Polity* 31 (3): 357–393.

Ghosh, Cyril. 2013. *The Politics of the American Dream: Democratic Inclusion in Contemporary American Political Culture*. New York: Palgrave Macmillan.

Henderson, Nia-Malika. 2014. "What President Obama Gets Wrong About 'Acting White.'" *The Washington Post*, July 24. https://www.washingtonpost.com/blogs/she-the-people/wp/2014/07/24/what-precb13de5ea251.

Horowitz, Paul. 2007. "Uncovering Identity." *Michigan Law Review* 105 (6): 1283–1300.

Kennedy, Anthony. 1993. Church of Lukumi Babalu Aye, Inc. v. City of Hialeah.

Lehring, Gary. 2003. *Officially Gay: The Political Construction of Sexuality*. Philadelphia: Temple University Press.

Scalia, Antonin. 1993. Church of Lukumi Babalu Aye, Inc. v. City of Hialeah.

Valdes, Francisco. 1995. "Queers, Sissies, Dykes and Tomboys: Deconstructing the Conflation of Sex, Gender and Sexual Orientation in Euro-American Law and Society." *California Law Review* 83 (1): 51–55.

Yoshino, Kenji. 2002. "Covering." *The Yale Law Journal* 111 (4): 769–939.

———. 2006. *Covering: The Hidden Assault on American Civil Rights*. New York: Random House.

Young, Iris Marion. 1990. *Justice and the Politics of Difference*. Princeton, NJ: Princeton University Press.

CHAPTER 5

Epilogue

Abstract In this epilogue, I offer some concluding remarks. These include an account of how I came to write this book, a discussion of my positionality, the challenges I encountered during the writing process, and my hopes regarding the future of this research.

Keywords Covering · Marriage equality · Pinkwashing · Positionality

I want to conclude with some remarks about my relationship to the critiques I have offered in this book. The discussions that appear here intersect with my own identity in ways that can—if I am not hyper-vigilant about it—compromise my ability to maintain a critical distance from the object of my inquiry. This is not to say I am always successful at the latter. But I do try very hard to remain mindful of this fact. But, then, such is always the plight of the social scientist. We are what we study. I have tried my best, however, to the extent possible, to offer a set of *disinterested* critiques here rather than a set of *interested* ones. While I cannot claim to be neutral (how can I? I am offering a polemic), I do hope I have written this book with a relatively clear sense of what constitutes fact and what constitutes value.

Let me also say a few things about my positionality: I am a queer-identified South Asian/Indian immigrant academic. I moved to the US in 2001. Ever since then I have frequently found myself being accused by some people of falling short of their expectations of me.

C. Ghosh, *De-Moralizing Gay Rights*,
https://doi.org/10.1007/978-3-319-78840-1_5

These criticisms are leveled at me in diverse ways but most of them belong to the same genus: You are not adequately performing your identities! Thus, I am routinely told that I am white-identified and that I am "acting straight" and that I am a "liberal" (as in a conservative, middle-of-the-road liberal) in that I am not adequately critical of US imperialism. I will set aside the accusation of being a race-betrayer for now because it is not a thematic issue I sufficiently address in this book. (I have only briefly engaged with it in Chapter 4.)

The other two utterances—that I am not sufficiently gay/queer-acting and that I endorse US imperialism—cause me a great deal of frustration. This is especially so because these remarks are typically made by people who are close to me in my personal life and my professional life. As a result, I routinely find myself explaining to these people why my conduct and my views do not, in fact, run contrary to my identity. At other times, I find myself justifying the political positions I have. And at yet other times, I find myself making mental notes that I should not care about these accusations even though they hurt quite a bit inasmuch as they deploy the twin barbs of disappointment and betrayal as I am made to understand that, *inter alia*: I have let down the homosexuals; and/or I have let down the brown-skinned/immigrants; and/or I have let down the lefties. I should emphasize this: the people who bring these charges against me are actually perfectly wonderful people. However, they do have a clear set of expectations about what a queer-identified immigrant from a former colony *should* have to say about politics—at least in an ideal world. I routinely find myself both inside and outside dominant discourses. And I remain committed to the eradication, or at least the chipping away, of the inside/outside binary.

This book and the investigations in it come out of my struggles with, and indeed dissent from, these criticisms of my views and my conduct. The polemic offered here is thus invested in a critical commitment to justice in the world but one that is always already ensconced in an ethic of dissent. I take it as axiomatic that there is a myriad of ways *to be.* And that this is a good thing in the world.

Thus, I am just as critical of pinkwashing and of US imperialism as the next person but I am also committed to preserving the semantic distinction between the two terms. The Global War on Terror has triggered a massive humanitarian crisis in western and southern Asia. It is a misguided, inhumane, and unwinnable war. Just as it did in Vietnam once, the US should pull back from western and southern Asia.

Israeli settlements, especially in the West Bank and East Jerusalem, and to smaller extent in the Golan Heights, stand in the way of a lasting resolution of the Arab–Israeli conflict in Israel–Palestine, and should therefore be dismantled. Sometimes pinkwashing can buttress these forms of imperialism, or neocolonialism if you will, but, as I have shown in Chapter 2, it does not always do so. It is also true that not all Israelis endorse the Israeli state's foreign policy and not everything the US does in the world is imperial.

I am just as critical of denying gays and lesbians the right to marry while preserving marriage as the exclusive prerogative of heterosexual couples as the next person. To this extent, I am in favor of marriage equality. But I am also committed to working toward dismantling a regime of state-endorsed intimacies where marriage is sanctified and those who cannot or will not marry are vilified. I am interested in forever expanding the range of family formations and not in curtailing it. This does not position me as someone who is opposed to gay rights. It positions me as someone who does not demean people who do not want, or cannot have in spite of wanting, one romantic partner who is also a spouse.

I am just as critical of covering demands as the next person but I also want to think about what it is that compels someone to cover. In so doing, I want to preserve the distinction between the agent placing the covering demand and the agent who is doing the covering. I take issue predominantly, if not exclusively, with the former. If I am committed to dismantling anything it is the covering demand itself and not the integrity of the person who has been swept up in its assimilationist injunctions.

•••

I will end with a remark about the future directions of the inquiries offered in this book. In Chapter 1, I mentioned that the critiques presented here are intended to change the tenor of contemporary LGBT+ rights discourse. They are intended as interruptions to monologues with a call to begin dialogues. They are not intended as final utterances on anything at all. I must reiterate that I sincerely mean this. I do hope some of the themes I have engaged with here are taken up by other scholars—fellow travelers who are on the same journey as I am on—who want to continue these conversations and, in so doing, also wish to refine them. This, I believe, would be a good thing! It is a matter of faith for me that my efforts in writing this book will have been rewarded if and only if the ideas presented here generate their own oppositions. This is how things should always be.

Appendix

Full Transcript of Secretary of State Hillary Clinton's Human Rights Day Speech, Delivered Today in Geneva. Text Posted with Permission from The White House Office of Communications (*Source *Text adapted from Clinton 2011)

Good evening, and let me express my deep honor and pleasure at being here. I want to thank Director General Tokayev and Ms. Wyden along with other ministers, ambassadors, excellencies, and UN partners. This weekend, we will celebrate Human Rights Day, the anniversary of one of the great accomplishments of the last century.

Beginning in 1947, delegates from six continents devoted themselves to drafting a declaration that would enshrine the fundamental rights and freedoms of people everywhere. In the aftermath of World War II, many nations pressed for a statement of this kind to help ensure that we would prevent future atrocities and protect the inherent humanity and dignity of all people. And so the delegates went to work. They discussed, they wrote, they revisited, revised, rewrote, for thousands of hours. And they incorporated suggestions and revisions from governments, organizations, and individuals around the world.

At three o'clock in the morning on December 10, 1948, after nearly two years of drafting and one last long night of debate, the president of the UN General Assembly called for a vote on the final text. Forty-eight nations voted in favor; eight abstained; none dissented. And the Universal Declaration of Human Rights was adopted. It proclaims a

C. Ghosh, *De-Moralizing Gay Rights*,
https://doi.org/10.1007/978-3-319-78840-1

simple, powerful idea: All human beings are born free and equal in dignity and rights. And with the declaration, it was made clear that rights are not conferred by government; they are the birthright of all people. It does not matter what country we live in, who our leaders are, or even who we are. Because we are human, we therefore have rights. And because we have rights, governments are bound to protect them.

In the 63 years since the declaration was adopted, many nations have made great progress in making human rights a human reality. Step by step, barriers that once prevented people from enjoying the full measure of liberty, the full experience of dignity, and the full benefits of humanity have fallen away. In many places, racist laws have been repealed, legal and social practices that relegated women to second-class status have been abolished, the ability of religious minorities to practice their faith freely has been secured.

In most cases, this progress was not easily won. People fought and organized and campaigned in public squares and private spaces to change not only laws, but hearts and minds. And thanks to that work of generations, for millions of individuals whose lives were once narrowed by injustice, they are now able to live more freely and to participate more fully in the political, economic, and social lives of their communities.

Now, there is still, as you all know, much more to be done to secure that commitment, that reality, and progress for all people. Today, I want to talk about the work we have left to do to protect one group of people whose human rights are still denied in too many parts of the world today. In many ways, they are an invisible minority. They are arrested, beaten, terrorized, even executed. Many are treated with contempt and violence by their fellow citizens while authorities empowered to protect them look the other way or, too often, even join in the abuse. They are denied opportunities to work and learn, driven from their homes and countries, and forced to suppress or deny who they are to protect themselves from harm.

I am talking about gay, lesbian, bisexual, and transgender people, human beings born free and given bestowed equality and dignity, who have a right to claim that, which is now one of the remaining human rights challenges of our time. I speak about this subject knowing that my own country's record on human rights for gay people is far from perfect. Until 2003, it was still a crime in parts of our country. Many LGBT Americans have endured violence and harassment in their own lives, and for some, including many young people, bullying and exclusion are daily experiences. So we, like all nations, have more work to do to protect human rights at home.

Now, raising this issue, I know, is sensitive for many people and that the obstacles standing in the way of protecting the human rights of LGBT people rest on deeply held personal, political, cultural, and religious beliefs. So I come here before you with respect, understanding, and humility. Even though progress on this front is not easy, we cannot delay acting. So in that spirit, I want to talk about the difficult and important issues we must address together to reach a global consensus that recognizes the human rights of LGBT citizens everywhere.

The first issue goes to the heart of the matter. Some have suggested that gay rights and human rights are separate and distinct; but, in fact, they are one and the same. Now, of course, 60 years ago, the governments that drafted and passed the Universal Declaration of Human Rights were not thinking about how it applied to the LGBT community. They also weren't thinking about how it applied to indigenous people or children or people with disabilities or other marginalized groups. Yet in the past 60 years, we have come to recognize that members of these groups are entitled to the full measure of dignity and rights, because, like all people, they share a common humanity.

This recognition did not occur all at once. It evolved over time. And as it did, we understood that we were honoring rights that people always had, rather than creating new or special rights for them. Like being a woman, like being a racial, religious, tribal, or ethnic minority, being LGBT does not make you less human. And that is why gay rights are human rights, and human rights are gay rights.

It is violation of human rights when people are beaten or killed because of their sexual orientation, or because they do not conform to cultural norms about how men and women should look or behave. It is a violation of human rights when governments declare it illegal to be gay, or allow those who harm gay people to go unpunished. It is a violation of human rights when lesbian or transgendered women are subjected to so-called corrective rape, or forcibly subjected to hormone treatments, or when people are murdered after public calls for violence toward gays, or when they are forced to flee their nations and seek asylum in other lands to save their lives. And it is a violation of human rights when life-saving care is withheld from people because they are gay, or equal access to justice is denied to people because they are gay, or public spaces are out of bounds to people because they are gay. No matter what we look like, where we come from, or who we are, we are all equally entitled to our human rights and dignity.

The second issue is a question of whether homosexuality arises from a particular part of the world. Some seem to believe it is a western phenomenon, and therefore people outside the West have grounds to reject it. Well, in reality, gay people are born into and belong to every society in the world. They are all ages, all races, all faiths; they are doctors and teachers, farmers and bankers, soldiers and athletes; and whether we know it, or whether we acknowledge it, they are our family, our friends, and our neighbors.

Being gay is not a western invention; it is a human reality. And protecting the human rights of all people, gay or straight, is not something that only western governments do. South Africa's constitution, written in the aftermath of Apartheid, protects the equality of all citizens, including gay people. In Colombia and Argentina, the rights of gays are also legally protected. In Nepal, the supreme court has ruled that equal rights apply to LGBT citizens. The Government of Mongolia has committed to pursue new legislation that will tackle anti-gay discrimination.

Now, some worry that protecting the human rights of the LGBT community is a luxury that only wealthy nations can afford. But in fact, in all countries, there are costs to not protecting these rights, in both gay and straight lives lost to disease and violence, and the silencing of voices and views that would strengthen communities, in ideas never pursued by entrepreneurs who happen to be gay. Costs are incurred whenever any group is treated as lesser or the other, whether they are women, racial, or religious minorities, or the LGBT. Former President Mogae of Botswana pointed out recently that for as long as LGBT people are kept in the shadows, there cannot be an effective public health program to tackle HIV and AIDS. Well, that holds true for other challenges as well.

The third, and perhaps most challenging, issue arises when people cite religious or cultural values as a reason to violate or not to protect the human rights of LGBT citizens. This is not unlike the justification offered for violent practices towards women like honor killings, widow burning, or female genital mutilation. Some people still defend those practices as part of a cultural tradition. But violence toward women isn't cultural; it's criminal. Likewise with slavery, what was once justified as sanctioned by God is now properly reviled as an unconscionable violation of human rights.

In each of these cases, we came to learn that no practice or tradition trumps the human rights that belong to all of us. And this holds true for inflicting violence on LGBT people, criminalizing their status or behavior, expelling them from their families and communities, or tacitly or explicitly accepting their killing.

Of course, it bears noting that rarely are cultural and religious traditions and teachings actually in conflict with the protection of human rights. Indeed, our religion and our culture are sources of compassion and inspiration toward our fellow human beings. It was not only those who've justified slavery who leaned on religion, it was also those who sought to abolish it. And let us keep in mind that our commitments to protect the freedom of religion and to defend the dignity of LGBT people emanate from a common source. For many of us, religious belief and practice is a vital source of meaning and identity, and fundamental to who we are as people. And likewise, for most of us, the bonds of love and family that we forge are also vital sources of meaning and identity. And caring for others is an expression of what it means to be fully human. It is because the human experience is universal that human rights are universal and cut across all religions and cultures.

The fourth issue is what history teaches us about how we make progress towards rights for all. Progress starts with honest discussion. Now, there are some who say and believe that all gay people are pedophiles, that homosexuality is a disease that can be caught or cured, or that gays recruit others to become gay. Well, these notions are simply not true. They are also unlikely to disappear if those who promote or accept them are dismissed out of hand rather than invited to share their fears and concerns. No one has ever abandoned a belief because he was forced to do so.

Universal human rights include freedom of expression and freedom of belief, even if our words or beliefs denigrate the humanity of others. Yet, while we are each free to believe whatever we choose, we cannot do whatever we choose, not in a world where we protect the human rights of all.

Reaching understanding of these issues takes more than speech. It does take a conversation. In fact, it takes a constellation of conversations in places big and small. And it takes a willingness to see stark differences in belief as a reason to begin the conversation, not to avoid it.

But progress comes from changes in laws. In many places, including my own country, legal protections have preceded, not followed, broader recognition of rights. Laws have a teaching effect. Laws that discriminate validate other kinds of discrimination. Laws that require equal protections reinforce the moral imperative of equality. And practically speaking, it is often the case that laws must change before fears about change dissipate.

Many in my country thought that President Truman was making a grave error when he ordered the racial desegregation of our military. They argued that it would undermine unit cohesion. And it wasn't until he went ahead and did it that we saw how it strengthened our social fabric in ways even the supporters of the policy could not foresee. Likewise, some worried in my country that the repeal of "Don't Ask, Don't Tell" would have a negative effect on our armed forces. Now, the Marine Corps Commandant, who was one of the strongest voices against the repeal, says that his concerns were unfounded and that the Marines have embraced the change.

Finally, progress comes from being willing to walk a mile in someone else's shoes. We need to ask ourselves, "How would it feel if it were a crime to love the person I love? How would it feel to be discriminated against for something about myself that I cannot change?" This challenge applies to all of us as we reflect upon deeply held beliefs, as we work to embrace tolerance and respect for the dignity of all persons, and as we engage humbly with those with whom we disagree in the hope of creating greater understanding.

A fifth and final question is how we do our part to bring the world to embrace human rights for all people including LGBT people. Yes, LGBT people must help lead this effort, as so many of you are. Their knowledge and experiences are invaluable and their courage inspirational. We know the names of brave LGBT activists who have literally given their lives for this cause, and there are many more whose names we will never know. But often those who are denied rights are least empowered to bring about the changes they seek. Acting alone, minorities can never achieve the majorities necessary for political change.

So when any part of humanity is sidelined, the rest of us cannot sit on the sidelines. Every time a barrier to progress has fallen, it has taken a cooperative effort from those on both sides of the barrier. In the fight for women's rights, the support of men remains crucial. The fight for racial equality has relied on contributions from people of all races. Combating Islamaphobia or anti-Semitism is a task for people of all faiths. And the same is true with this struggle for equality.

Conversely, when we see denials and abuses of human rights and fail to act, that sends the message to those deniers and abusers that they won't suffer any consequences for their actions, and so they carry on. But when we do act, we send a powerful moral message. Right here in Geneva, the international community acted this year to strengthen a global consensus around the human rights of LGBT people. At the Human Rights Council in March, 85 countries from all regions supported a statement calling for an end to criminalization and violence against people because of their sexual orientation and gender identity.

At the following session of the Council in June, South Africa took the lead on a resolution about violence against LGBT people. The delegation from South Africa spoke eloquently about their own experience and struggle for human equality and its indivisibility. When the measure passed, it became the first-ever UN resolution recognizing the human rights of gay people worldwide. In the Organization of American States this year, the Inter-American Commission on Human Rights created a unit on the rights of LGBT people, a step toward what we hope will be the creation of a special rapporteur.

Now, we must go further and work here and in every region of the world to galvanize more support for the human rights of the LGBT community. To the leaders of those countries where people are jailed, beaten, or executed for being gay, I ask you to consider this: Leadership, by definition, means being out in front of your people when it is called for. It means standing up for the dignity of all your citizens and persuading your people to do the same. It also means ensuring that all citizens are treated as equals under your laws, because let me be clear—I am not saying that gay people can't or don't commit crimes. They can and they do, just like straight people. And when they do, they should be held accountable, but it should never be a crime to be gay.

And to people of all nations, I say supporting human rights is your responsibility too. The lives of gay people are shaped not only by laws, but by the treatment they receive every day from their families, from their neighbors. Eleanor Roosevelt, who did so much to advance human rights worldwide, said that these rights begin in the small places close to home—the streets where people live, the schools they attend, the factories, farms, and offices where they work. These places are your domain. The actions you take, the ideals that you advocate, can determine whether human rights flourish where you are.

And finally, to LGBT men and women worldwide, let me say this: Wherever you live and whatever the circumstances of your life, whether you are connected to a network of support or feel isolated and vulnerable, please know that you are not alone. People around the globe are working hard to support you and to bring an end to the injustices and dangers you face. That is certainly true for my country. And you have an ally in the United States of America and you have millions of friends among the American people.

The Obama Administration defends the human rights of LGBT people as part of our comprehensive human rights policy and as a priority of our foreign policy. In our embassies, our diplomats are raising concerns about specific cases and laws, and working with a range of partners to strengthen human rights protections for all. In Washington, we have created a task force at the State Department to support and coordinate this work. And in the coming months, we will provide every embassy with a toolkit to help improve their efforts. And we have created a program that offers emergency support to defenders of human rights for LGBT people.

This morning, back in Washington, President Obama put into place the first U.S. Government strategy dedicated to combating human rights abuses against LGBT persons abroad. Building on efforts already underway at the State Department and across the government, the President has directed all U.S. Government agencies engaged overseas to combat the criminalization of LGBT status and conduct, to enhance efforts to protect vulnerable LGBT refugees and asylum seekers, to ensure that our foreign assistance promotes the protection of LGBT rights, to enlist international organizations in the fight against discrimination, and to respond swiftly to abuses against LGBT persons.

I am also pleased to announce that we are launching a new Global Equality Fund that will support the work of civil society organizations working on these issues around the world. This fund will help them record facts so they can target their advocacy, learn how to use the law as a tool, manage their budgets, train their staffs, and forge partnerships with women's organizations and other human rights groups. We have committed more than $3 million to start this fund, and we have hope that others will join us in supporting it.

The women and men who advocate for human rights for the LGBT community in hostile places, some of whom are here today with us, are brave and dedicated, and deserve all the help we can give them. We know the road ahead will not be easy. A great deal of work lies before us.

But many of us have seen firsthand how quickly change can come. In our lifetimes, attitudes toward gay people in many places have been transformed. Many people, including myself, have experienced a deepening of our own convictions on this topic over the years, as we have devoted more thought to it, engaged in dialogues and debates, and established personal and professional relationships with people who are gay.

This evolution is evident in many places. To highlight one example, the Delhi High Court decriminalized homosexuality in India two years ago, writing, and I quote, “If there is one tenet that can be said to be an underlying theme of the Indian constitution, it is inclusiveness.” There is little doubt in my mind that support for LGBT human rights will continue to climb. Because for many young people, this is simple: All people deserve to be treated with dignity and have their human rights respected, no matter who they are or whom they love.

There is a phrase that people in the United States invoke when urging others to support human rights: “Be on the right side of history.” The story of the United States is the story of a nation that has repeatedly grappled with intolerance and inequality. We fought a brutal civil war over slavery. People from coast to coast joined in campaigns to recognize the rights of women, indigenous peoples, racial minorities, children, people with disabilities, immigrants, workers, and on and on. And the march toward equality and justice has continued. Those who advocate for expanding the circle of human rights were and are on the right side of history, and history honors them. Those who tried to constrict human rights were wrong, and history reflects that as well.

I know that the thoughts I’ve shared today involve questions on which opinions are still evolving. As it has happened so many times before, opinion will converge once again with the truth, the immutable truth, that all persons are created free and equal in dignity and rights. We are called once more to make real the words of the Universal Declaration. Let us answer that call. Let us be on the right side of history, for our people, our nations, and future generations, whose lives will be shaped by the work we do today. I come before you with great hope and confidence that no matter how long the road ahead, we will travel it successfully together. Thank you very much.

Reference

Clinton, Hillary. 2011. "Hillary Clinton on Gay Rights Abroad: Secretary of State Delivers Historic LGBT Speech in Geneva (Video, Full Text)." December 6. https://www.huffingtonpost.com/2011/12/06/hillary-clinton-gay-rights-speech-geneva_n_1132392.html.

Index

A
"acting straight", 77–79, 88, 96
"acting white", 7, 78, 79, 92
Afghanistan, 17, 20
Agathangelou, Anna, 23–25, 33
amatonormativity, 2, 6, 8, 45–47, 51, 52, 65. *See also* love
American Jeremiad. *See* Jeremiad
anatomy, 5

B
Baehr v. Lewin, 63
Baehr v. Miike. See Baehr v. Lewin
Baker v. State of Vermont, 63
bathroom bills. *See* transgender
Berlant, Lauren, 3
binary logic, 2, 12
black civil rights movement. *See* civil rights
Brake, Elizabeth, 47
Butler, Judith, 4, 79, 82

C
children, 2, 6, 8, 23, 29, 30, 34, 45, 46, 51–56, 65
chromosomes, 5
Church of Lukumi Babalu Aye v. City of Hialeah, 88
civil rights, 34, 65, 74–76, 89
classism, 85
Clinton, Hillary Rodham, 22–32, 34, 35
concepts, 8, 18, 92
  concept-clarification, 84
  essentially contested, 92
constructionism, 4, 66
context, 3–5, 7, 11, 12, 17, 19, 27, 28, 30, 33, 48, 51–53, 57, 59, 65, 74, 75, 77–79, 81, 90, 91
  discursive, 4, 13, 28
conversion, 7, 21, 75
covering, 2, 7, 8, 74–81, 84–92, 97
critical race theory, 89
cultural imperialism, 47, 51, 52
culture, 6, 18, 46, 50, 51, 56, 74, 77, 80, 84–88, 92

C. Ghosh, *De-Moralizing Gay Rights*,
https://doi.org/10.1007/978-3-319-78840-1

D
decisional minimalism, 6, 45, 56, 59, 62, 65
democratic inclusion, 3. *See also* identity politics
desire, 5, 7, 56, 81, 88
difference. *See* identity politics
disability studies. *See* identity politics
discourse, 2–5, 12, 26, 28, 61, 65, 75, 97. *See also* context
dissent, 4, 66, 96
diversity. *See* identity politics
Don't Ask, Don't Tell, 20, 29, 81, 92
due process, 60
Duggan, Lisa, 25
dyad, 46–48, 51, 52. *See also* love; binary logics

E
Egypt, 17
equal protection, 30, 60, 62, 63, 67
essentialism, strategic, 38
ethnic studies. *See* identity politics

F
feminism. *See* identity politics
fertility, 66
Fire Island, 87, 88, 91
Foucault, Michel, 4
Franke, Katherine, 6, 13, 14, 36, 50, 92
Fraser, Nancy, 3, 8, 37, 65, 74, 92
Fuss, Diana, 4

G
gay and lesbian studies, 3
gender identity, 21, 23, 27, 31, 77
Ginsburg, Ruth Bader (Justice), 62
Global War on Terror, 12, 13, 34, 96
Goffman, Erving, 74
Goodridge v. Dept. of Public Health, 63
Griswold v. Connecticut, 62
grooming. *See* civil rights
Gross, Aeyal, 14, 35

H
hegemony, 4, 5
heteronormativity, 45, 51–52
heterosexuality, 3, 4, 8, 30, 97
homonationalism, 18, 19, 28, 33
homonormativity, 2, 25, 28, 66. *See also* amatonormativity; repronormativity
homosexuality, 4, 27, 32, 77
hypocrisy, 26, 58, 59

I
identification, 86
identity politics, 3, 32, 46, 57, 58, 65, 66, 74, 78, 85, 103. *See also* multiculturalism
imperialism, 13, 20–22, 25, 26, 33–35, 47, 51, 52, 96, 97
  cultural, 47, 51, 52
Islam, 6, 12–18, 20–23, 32, 33, 35, 37
Islamophobia. *See* Islam
Israel, 6, 13, 14, 17, 22, 29, 35, 37, 87, 97

J
Jagose, Annamarie, 3
Jeremiad, 2

K
Kennedy, Anthony (Justice), 44

L
Lawrence v. Texas, 38, 60, 62, 67
love, 28, 45–49, 51, 52, 66, 76, 81, 97
Loving v. Viriginia, 60

M
Masterpiece Cakeshop v. Colorado Civil Rights Commission, 65
Metz, Tamara, 50
Middle East. *See* West Asia
misrecognition, 8, 31, 92
Mission Creep, 12, 36
möbius strip, 2, 20
multiculturalism, 3, 32
Mungin, Lawrence, 90
Muslims. *See* Islam

N
Namaste, Ki, 4
nationalism, 33, 35
New Left, 3
norm, 5, 45, 49, 52, 56, 77, 78

O
Obama, Barack, 20, 22, 26, 28, 36, 64, 92
Obergefell v. Hodges, 2, 6, 44, 66
oppression, 7, 13, 23, 32, 36, 37, 65
originalism, 61

P
Palestine, 17, 37, 97
passing, 78, 79
performativity, 82
politics, 2, 3, 5, 6, 12, 15, 16, 20, 21, 33, 57, 65, 96. *See also* identity politics
  of acknowledgment, 3
  of difference, 3
  emancipatory, 2
  of identity, 3. *See also* identity politics
  radical, 2, 5, 33, 57
  of recognition, 3
polyamory, 66
positionality, 95
poststructuralism, 3
pregnancy, 75
privacy, 60, 62
Puar, Jasbir, 15, 16
public reason, 58, 59, 66

Q
quirkyalones, 49

R
race, 23, 27, 60, 74, 75, 77, 79, 89–91, 96
Radical Theory Creep, 6, 12, 13, 15, 17, 22, 24, 25, 34, 35
realpolitik, 58
repronormativity, 1, 2, 6, 8, 28, 43, 45–46, 51–54, 65. *See also* children
rhetoric, 2, 5, 8, 12, 13, 15, 25, 36, 65
  metonymy, 32
  moralizing, 2, 5, 7
Roe v. Wade, 62
romance. *See* love
Romania, 14, 16, 19, 32
Rosen, Jeffrey, 62

S
Scalia, Antonin (Justice), 66
Schulman, Sarah, 6, 13, 14
Sedgwick, Eve Kosofsky, 5

Seneca Falls Convention, 34
sex characteristics, 5
sexual exclusivity, 49
sexuality, 4, 5, 7, 24, 46, 51, 60
sexual minorities, 33, 60, 83
sexual orientation, 5, 21, 23, 27, 31, 74, 77, 83
singlism, 47. *See also* heteronormativity
slavery, 23, 34
social justice, 3. *See also* identity politics
sodomy laws, 26–28, 30, 38, 60
Spade, Dean, 20, 36
stigma, 53, 54, 74
Sunstein, Cass, 6, 45, 56, 59, 62

T
textualism, 61
transgender, 31, 64, 100, 101
Tribe, Laurence, 38, 60

U
United Nations High Commissioner for Refugees (UNHCR), 37
United Nations, 22, 37, 61
United States v. Windsor, 44
United Nations Relief and Works Agency for Palestine Refugees in the Near East (UNRWA), 37
US Congress, 21, 62

W
Warner, Michael, 3, 26, 46, 49, 66
Weber, Cynthia, 12, 25, 35
West Asia, 14, 17
women's studies, 3. *See also* identity politics
work–family balance, 52. *See also* heteronormativity
work–life balance, 52. *See also* heteronormativity

Y
Yoshino, Kenji, 2, 7, 74
Young, Iris Marion, 47

CPSIA information can be obtained
at www.ICGtesting.com
Printed in the USA
LVHW03*1957111018
593276LV00010B/212/P

9 783319 788395